Lewis Coolidge and
the Voyage of the Amethyst

1806–1811

Studies in Maritime History
William N. Still, Jr., Series Editor

RECENT TITLES

Iron Afloat:
The Story of the Confederate Armorclads
William N. Still, Jr.

To California by Sea:
A Maritime History of the Gold Rush
James P. Delgado

Lifeline of the Confederacy:
Blockade Running during the Civil War
Stephen R. Wise

The Lure of Neptune:
German-Soviet Naval Collaboration
and Ambitions
Tobias R. Philbin III

High Seas Confederate:
The Life and Times of
John Newland Maffitt
Royce Shingleton

The Defeat of the German U-Boats:
The Battle of the Atlantic
David Syrett

John P. Holland, 1841–1914:
Inventor of the Modern Submarine
Richard Knowles Morris

Cockburn and the British Navy in Transition:
Admiral Sir George Cockburn, 1772–1853
Roger Morriss

The Royal Navy in European Waters
during the American Revolutionary War
David Syrett

Sir John Fisher's Naval Revolution
Nicholas A. Lambert

Forty-Niners 'round the Horn
Charles R. Schultz

The Abandoned Ocean
Andrew Gibson and Arthur Donovan

Northern Naval Superiority and the
Economics of the American Civil War
David G. Surdam

Ironclads and Big Guns of the Confederacy:
The Journal and Letters of John M. Brooke
Edited by George M. Brooke, Jr.

High Seas and Yankee Gunboats:
A Blockade-Running Adventure from the
Diary of James Dickson
Roger S. Durham

Dead Men Tell No Tales:
The Lives and Legends of the
Pirate Charles Gibbs
Joseph Gibbs

Playships of the World:
The Naval Diaries of Admiral Dan Gallery,
1920–1924
Edited by Robert Shenk

Lewis Coolidge and the Voyage of the
Amethyst, 1806–1811
Evabeth Miller Kienast and
John Phillip Felt

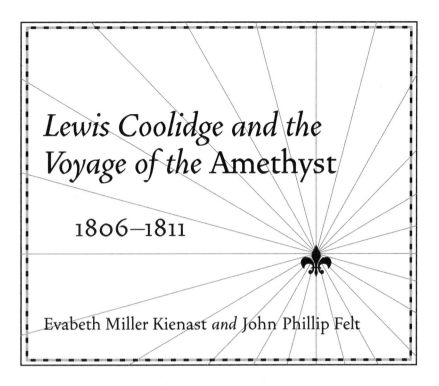

Lewis Coolidge and the
Voyage of the Amethyst

1806–1811

Evabeth Miller Kienast *and* John Phillip Felt

THE UNIVERSITY OF SOUTH CAROLINA PRESS

Coauthor John Phillip Felt is a retired senior foreign officer of the United States Department of State. The opinions and characterizations in this book are those of the author and do not necessarily represent official positions of the United States government.

Published by the University of South Carolina Press
Columbia, South Carolina 29208

www.sc.edu/uscpress

Manufactured in the United States of America

18 17 16 15 14 13 12 11 10 09   10 9 8 7 6 5 4 3 2 1

Library of Congress Cataloging-in-Publication Data

Kienast, Evabeth Miller, 1912–2007.
    Lewis Coolidge and the voyage of the Amethyst, 1806–1811 / Evabeth Miller Kienast and John Phillip Felt.
        p. cm. — (Studies in maritime history)
    Includes bibliographical references and index.
        ISBN 978-1-57003-816-7 (cloth : alk. paper)
    1. Sealing—United States—History—19th century—Sources. 2. Fur trade—United States—History—19th century—Sources. 3. Fur trade—China—History—19th century—Sources. 4. Coolidge, Lewis, 1783–1872—Diaries. 5. Coolidge, Lewis, 1783–1872—Travel. 6. Merchant mariners—United States—Diaries. 7. Farmers—United States—Diaries. 8. Amethyst (Ship)—History—Sources. I. Felt, John Phillip, 1944– II. Title.
    SH361.K54 2009
    910.9164—dc22

                              2008049197

This book was printed on Glatfelter Natures, a recycled paper with 30 percent postconsumer waste content.

CONTENTS

Illustrations

Preface

Lewis Coolidge's grandchildren told me that he was an impractical man, more interested in beautiful sunsets and poetry than in running his farm in Illinois. Yet that may be why he takes on a certain immortality here on earth, beyond that of other pioneers buried in the quiet Jubilee churchyard.

These elderly grandchildren remembered him for the wonderful stories he told as they sat around the Franklin stove in their farm home and for the long letters he often wrote "back east" to relatives in Boston, but they were amazed at the remarkable journal they found of his global voyage aboard the *Amethyst*, just as the War of 1812 was brewing.

Yet such a flair for adventure might have been expected from a nephew of Billy Dawes, the daring young partner of Paul Revere, whose part in the famous midnight ride was finally given its due in Esther Forbes's Pulitzer Prize–winning book, *Paul Revere and the World He Lived In*. From 1806 to 1811, Lewis Coolidge sailed around the world on a sealing expedition, spending most of that time in the Pacific waters that so many other American young men came to know well after the Japanese attack on Pearl Harbor in 1941. His adventures included a long stay in the Philippines, and he described Manila and the life and customs of that time in detail, mentioning places that still bear names very like those he used. His impressions and descriptions were sometimes lofty, sometimes rather spicy.

Some of the incidents recounted remind one of those described thirty years later in Herman Melville's *Typee*. This likeness is interesting in light of the fact that Coolidge's diary was never published and therefore was probably not seen by anyone outside his family, and also because the private diarist of no literary pretension observed and described native life in much the same way as did Melville, the professional writer.

Young Lewis Coolidge told all in his sea journal—the killing of an albatross, which some may regard as the reason that he was the only one of the ship' s company to get back to Boston; his awakening to the brutality of life at sea, which he had expected to be noble; his year-long stay on one island, caring for scurvy-scourged men; the crew's celebration of the Fourth of July on a rocky island near Baja California, when the United States of America was little more than thirty years old; the sailors' adventures and amours among the native tribes of the South Seas; their avoidance of Spanish pirate ships and English vessels; his visit to St. Helena several years before Napoleon's exile there; and his frank opinions of everything, everywhere.

The journal was written with a quill pen in a hand so fine that reading it requires use of a magnifying glass. With a few old letters it stayed for many years among the family papers in Illinois, regarded only as a curiosity of interest to no one but the Coolidge relatives. It was their only tangible memento of Lewis Coolidge's travels, for he had told them that his collection of curios had been confiscated when he was impressed by the British on arriving in Boston Harbor. Interviewed by a newspaper reporter on her career as a nurse, the late Miss Eleanor Coolidge, aged granddaughter of this Boston voyageur, happened to mention the old diary. It was brought down from a closet shelf, and so began its editing for a later Yankee generation, to which World War II and ensuing events had given vivid reality to Lewis Coolidge's itinerary.

Lewis Coolidge was born in Boston on September 16, 1783, just two weeks after the treaty signing in Paris brought an official end to the American colonies' war for independence. He died eighty-eight years later, in Brimfield, Illinois, on October 19, 1871. His father, Lieutenant John Coolidge, was kin to ancestors of President Calvin Coolidge. His mother was Lydia Dawes, sister of that intrepid Billy who disguised himself to carry messages for the rebellious colonists. An exquisite wax portrait in profile is treasured by the family as an almost "speaking likeness" of Lydia.

Lewis had an academy education, says family tradition, but there is no mention of his having gone further in his studies, although it was not until the day after his twenty-third birthday that he set out on his five-year voyage. After his return and his escape from the British, he served as a private in Jonathan Whitney's company of the second regiment of the Massachusetts Militia.

He went up to Vermont later to teach school, and there at Waltham in 1818 he married Amanda Mills Dennison, a practical woman who went west with him and their children in 1834 to settle on the Peoria County prairie. They lived near the site soon to be chosen by Bishop Philander Chase, Episcopal divine, for his Jubilee College, which is today an Illinois state park. Here Lewis Coolidge tried to farm, but it developed that his son Edward, "a stout athletic youth, my main defendour," was better suited to that task, and he gradually took over the entire responsibility. Amanda, meanwhile, operated an inn where the stage passengers riding between Galesburg and Peoria stopped to devour her chicken dinners with great relish.

ELEANOR COOLIDGE . . . Eleanor Coolidge has had a busy lifetime, crowded to the brim with the routine of hospitals and large institutions . . . soon after finishing her training at the Illinois Training school in Chicago, John Proctor asked her to take charge of the Proctor hospital, then known as the Cottage hospital . . . later she was in charge of the Proctor home for 24 years, and when the Buehler Home was opened she was in charge of it . . . retired now, "Aunt Nell" helps in the housekeeping and reads much . . . she admits being a "rocking chair farmer," reads the farm magazines and would like to live on a farm again . . . born on a farm near Brimfield, one of the bright spots of her childhood were the tales her grandfather, Lewis Coolidge used to tell her of his early adventures in sailing around Cape Horn, being held as a hostage by Spaniards and of the daily happenings aboard a sealing expedition . . . he also could quote Shakespeare by the hour . . . a member of the same Coolidge as our late president, Calvin Coolidge . . . Aunt Nell and her sister, "Aunt Em" lives at 207 South Garfield avenue.

Photograph and biography of Eleanor (Nell) Coolidge.
Courtesy of the *Peoria Journal Star*, 1942

Bishop Philander Chase,
founder of Kenyon College
and Jubilee College. Lithograph
portrait by Charles Overall.
Courtesy of Jubilee State Park

The inn guests were doubtless regaled by the little old gentleman whom they called "Captain Coolidge" with tales of his world wanderings and the heathen he had seen. And doubtless they told each other that their host was probably making up much of what he said, for such exotic places were far more fabulous to Middle Westerners than to seafaring New Englanders.

When he was sixty, Lewis Coolidge wrote to a nephew in Boston of his leisurely life, clearly sharing why his family considered him impractical but revealing as interesting a personality as the prairie could boast in 1843. "I am the last who gets up in the morning," he wrote, telling how Emma, his youngest daughter, "always waits to eat breakfast with me, combs my head, and is 'artful in the artlessness' to please me." He went on to praise the nobility of rural life, saying: "Pardon my severity on the City. I ever disliked it, altho I drew my first breath in it. I despise its aristocracy of wealth and its consequent sycophancy. I positively would prefer a lodgment among the rocky mountains than to be obliged to reside in Beacon Street."

Of an artist nephew joining in the famous Brook Farm experiment of communal living, he wrote:

> I rec'd a letter from Frank about two months since. It was obviously written under some aberration of mind. It is dated "Brook's Farm" which I suppose in plain parlance means a place for the insane! a sterile seclusion indeed, producing, if any, the most bitter fruit. He observes, "We live as

Edward Coolidge (1825–1904),
the son of Lewis Coolidge and
Amanda Denison

We please, do what We please, and dress as We please. I have adopted
a green and black plaid, as I think my ancestors were from Scotland and
have chosen as an employment drawing and designing. . . . I like this place
much, we live all in common, male and female." Poor fellow! I am induced
to wish that he was in another and better World.

Having thus contradicted the youthful idealism that had long before sent him
around the world in quest of noble adventure, he went on to describe Bishop
Chase's newly built chapel at Jubilee, which to this day possesses the same
beauty of surroundings that must have charmed him then:

It is very reasonable that an institution, and Chapel of this Kind, must
tend to introduce a more refin'd Society among us. . . . We have the delight
of hearing in these solitudes the "sweet Sabbath bell" and every day at
morning and evening prayer the solemn sound floats sweetly over the
Woods. A more enchanting situation for a Seminary and chapel cannot
be imagin'd. It is Situated on high ground, surrounded by romantic conical bluffs, and ancient Oaks, with the Kickapoo "winding its devious Way"
in front. here, but a few Years ago, these solemn Shades were only trodden

by the roving Indian. . . . About two Years past I cut an avenue thro the woods So as to have a view of the Chapel . . . this view thro the Woods of nearly a mile in extent is very greatly admired. it cost me a great deal of labour, but I am abundantly repaid. nothing you have around Boston is half so romantic. at the distance seen, the Chapel Appears like an Abbey or ancient Castle.

This Bostonian had even given up his liberal inclination to the Unitarian Church and was by this time a warden in the Episcopal parish there at Jubilee. He still used nautical language, however, advising that it was time for a certain kinsman "to heave his Mainsail to the Mast, retire, and live rusticly." That was just what Lewis Coolidge himself had done, but although he lived rustically, his lively letters show that even in isolation he never lost the sensitivity to life that had long before made him at home in far, strange places.

EVABETH MILLER KIENAST

New York City, 1942

ACKNOWLEDGMENTS

This edition is dedicated with great respect and affection to Evabeth Miller Kienast, who after more than a half-century of devotion to the resurrection of figures of history, passed away during the final drafting of this work. Evabeth was supported and inspired by her late husband, Dr. Hansjuergen Kienast, and her family. A dedicated genealogist, she retained until the end a vibrant interest in family history, particularly that of her Dinsmor and Langdon ancestors. Evabeth's attention to this story was first inspired by a colleague of hers at the *Peoria Journal Star*, Ruth Robertson, who piqued Evabeth's interest in Lewis Coolidge's adventures aboard the *Amethyst*. It was Ruth who was first shown the Lewis Coolidge diary in 1942 by Eleanor Coolidge and immediately brought the work to Evabeth's attention. Evabeth's early devotion to the transcription and study of the original text during the waning days of World War II laid the groundwork for the publication of this volume so many years later.

John Phillip Felt wishes to acknowledge first and foremost the contributions of Judy Clark Felt, "the wife of his youth who abides with him still." He and Judy's daughter, Emily Clemens Felt, and son, Justin Ennis Felt, provided constant encouragement and continuing faith that the project would end successfully. He also wishes to mention his uncle, Austin Vincent Felt, who provided an early interest in family history and transcribed Lewis Coolidge's 1843 letter, which appears in appendix B. His late great-aunt Eleanor Coolidge kept alive an interest in the adventures of her grandfather Lewis Coolidge.

Charles J. Frey, special collections librarian, Cullom-Davis Library, Bradley University, has provided a comfortable, secure home for the original journal of Lewis Coolidge and his original 1843 letter. David Pawson of the Smithsonian Institution provided valuable insights into the nature and value of sea cucumbers. Eric Grinsted, chief librarian, Library of the Daughters of the American Revolution, was a regular source of very sound advice on genealogy and family history. Melanie Tossell, Christine Michelini, and Irene Axelrod of the Peabody Essex Institute provided valuable assistance on China trade research and illustrations. Ray Winslow provided valuable guidance on computer applications. Brian Marquis provided graphic arts expertise in the form of the map of the route of the *Amethyst* on page xx.

Finally, Mr. Felt would like to express his gratitude to Alex Moore and Bill Adams of the University of South Carolina Press—advisers, editors, counselors—who, along with the dedicated staff of the press, helped bring this work to publication. Deborah Patton produced a very professional index.

Lewis Coolidge

Introduction

When Evabeth Miller Kienast wrote her 1942 preface to this book, there was interest from our military establishment in information about Palau. The Japanese had already bombed Pearl Harbor, and World War II was well under way. Some farsighted individuals saw the need for details about South Sea Islands for possible confrontations with Japan in that theater, such details as might come from even a very dated personal account like Lewis Coolidge's. However, Lewis Coolidge's journal of his 1806–1811 voyage aboard the *Amethyst* did not reach the appropriate authorities during World War II, and even if there was usable information in the journal, our forces succeeded without it in several battles in Palau in 1944.

As Ms. Kienast noted, Lewis Coolidge was well suited to be an observer and commentator in his long voyage to exotic places. He was well educated for his times, as can be seen in the many literary references sprinkled throughout his journal. Ms. Kienast and I have made every effort to repeat Lewis Coolidge's words without change. The spelling, punctuation, and expressions are his, with one exception. We have italicized the names of ships to ease identification and to conform to standard convention. Coolidge's position on the *Amethyst* was probably somewhere around the Second and Third Mates and experienced Able Seamen. He apparently had a comfortable relationship with Captain Smith and Chief Officer Carr yet always referred to Carr and Dorr, the supercargo (and relative of the owner), as "Mr. Carr" and "Mr. Dorr" respectively. He referred to all others by their full names rather than as Mr. So-and-so. Thus Coolidge was probably a member of the crew, but a senior one.

The registry for the *Amethyst* on this voyage, included as an illustration on page xxvi, notes the Dorrs as owners of the *Amethyst*. As Ebeneezer Dorr, Jr., was aboard the *Amethyst* during the entire voyage, it was a reasonably simple matter to sell the vessel in Canton, as stated on page 58. Dorr could have authorized it on the spot. At the very end of his journal, Lewis Coolidge wrote that he was the only one to return. He must have meant "the only one of the crew," as we read from his journal that he returned with Capt. Smith and Mr. Dorr.

The *Amethyst* was classed as a "ship" rather than a brigantine, brig, hermaphrodite brig, cutter, clipper, and so on. *Webster's New Collegiate Dictionary* defines *ship* first as "any large seagoing vessel . . . one not propelled by oars, paddles or the like." A succeeding definition refers to the specific nautical category of "ship": "a vessel with a bowsprit and three masts (foremast, mainmast, and mizzenmast) and, rarely a fourth mast, each composed of a lower mast, a topmast, and a topgallant mast, and, sometimes, higher masts." According to its registration papers (see page xxvi), the *Amethyst* was a square-sterned ship built in Salem in 1801 by Enos Briggs.[1] She had two decks, three masts, no galleries, and a figurehead. Her length was ninety-five feet six inches, her width twenty-five feet three inches, and her depth twelve feet seven and one-half inches. She drew two hundred seventy tons. She likely resembled the *Friendship of Salem*, a replica of which is the illustration on page 3.

On several successive registrations beginning in 1802, her ownership remained within the Dorr family but was transferred within the family. She passed from Andrew C. Dorr, Joseph Dorr, and John Dorr (1802) to John Dorr, Joseph Dorr, Andrew C. Dorr, Ebeneezer Dorr, Jr., and William Dorr (1803) to John Dorr and Joseph Dorr (1805). When the *Amethyst* began her 1806 voyage with Lewis Coolidge aboard, her ownership was listed only to Andrew C. Dorr, but Ebeneeer Dorr, Jr., was aboard as owner representative the entire voyage.

In *Boston Men on the Northwest Coast: The American Maritime Fur Trade, 1788–1844*, Mary Malloy writes of voyages of the *Amethyst* to the northwestern coast of North America:

> *Amethyst*
> This ship of 270 tons is presumed to have made three voyages to the Northwest Coast between 1802 and 1812. Built by Enos Briggs of Salem and launched in 1801, the 95-foot *Amethyst* returned to Boston in April 1803 from her first voyage to Canton, and is reckoned to have been on the Northwest Coast. Captain Jonathan Bowers was in command and the vessel was owned by Andrew, Joseph and John Dorr of Boston. The ship was registered again upon her return and Ebenezer, Jr. and William Dorr joined their kinsmen as owners. For the next six years the *Amethyst* was owned by one or more of the Dorrs. In 1805 the vessel was registered with Seth Smith as master and under his command left Boston in September 1806 for a sealing voyage around Cape Horn. The cabin boy of the *Amethyst* was described as a "N.W. Indian" who was sick with fits in October 1806, apparently having signed on in Boston. In May 1807 at Cedros Island, on the coast of California, the *Amethyst* picked up an American

and two Northwest Coast Indians left there by Captain Winship of the *O'Cain* to "collect sea otter skins."

The vessel was in Manila early in 1809 and in Canton a year later without having visited the northwest coast proper. More cruising in the Pacific was apparently suspended because the ship was in bad condition and unable to sail (as reported by Second Mate Ebenezer Dorr and others). According to the logbook, the ship was sold to Peter Dobell for $6,000 and the hands discharged in Whampoa in August 1810. Nonetheless, Dutch East India Company records report the vessel in Canton again (and again under the command of Seth Smith) in July 1811. That summer, Thomas Meek of Marblehead, Massachusetts, took command of the vessel from Smith in Canton and sailed for Sitka, where he arrived November. There Meek entered into an agreement with Alexander Baranov to carry Russian-contracted native Alaskan hunters and their fifty-two baidarkas to the coast of California. Three other Boston vessels were then involved in the same trade: the *Katherine,* the *Charon,* and the *Mercury,* which was, as the *Amethyst* had been, owned by members of the Dorr family. The ships left Sitka in January 1812 and proceeded down the coast, where they hunted through August. Late in the summer they returned to Sitka, where the *Amethyst* was eventually purchased by the Russians.[2]

The *Amethyst's* crew was engaged in the "Old China Trade," meaning trade prior to the First Opium War, which concluded in the 1840s. In the "Old China Trade," all international transactions were carried out through the port of Canton via a selected group of private Chinese traders known as "Hongs." The *Amethyst's* crew faced a problem familiar to the other "Yankee traders": finding commodities that would have a market in Canton that would provide revenue to purchase the silks, porcelain, tea, and so forth that would bring high prices back in Boston. The *Amethyst* focused primarily on fur seal skins and on sea cucumbers, as discussed in more detail in chapter 2.

The bibliography contains many excellent sources for readers who want to read more history about this trade. American literature also has a number of fictionalized accounts that add a measure of flavor not always found in the history texts. James Fenimore Cooper wrote his novel *The Sea Lions,* also called *The Lost Sealers,* in 1843, so it was a contemporary treatment of fur sealing. Cooper went to sea "before the mast" on a merchantman, not a sealer, at sixteen and later spent several years as an officer in the U.S. Navy. He was well prepared to write about the sea.

Herman Melville shipped on several Pacific whaling voyages in the 1840s and was familiar with the South Sea Islands he wrote of in *Typee, Omoo, Mardi, White-Jacket,* and of course, *Moby-Dick.* His short novel *Benito Cereno* is about an uprising on a slave ship, but the title character, loosely based on Captain Amasa Delano, a distant relative of President Franklin Delano Roosevelt, was a sealer. Melville's experience at sea and familiarity with the trading environment undoubtedly brought him an awareness of the fur sealing industry. This was evidenced in Andrew Delbanco's excellent 2005 biography, *Melville: His World and Work,* where Delbanco writes about Melville's novel *Israel Potter,* "in which he [Melville] described the Yankee defenders at Bunker Hill gripping their muskets by the barrel and beating back the British assault by 'wielding the stock right and left, as seal hunters on the beach knock down with their clubs the Shetland seal.'"[3]

Richard Henry Dana's classic, *Two Years before the Mast,* was nonfiction and contained numerous comparisons to Lewis Coolidge's journal. Dana's sea voyage took place from 1834 to 1836 after fur sealing had declined. Dana and his shipmates focused on Californian cattle hides for the market in New England, rather than the China market.

In 1892, in a time of resurgence in the fur seal industry, Jack London shipped on "the *Sophia Sunderland,* a three-hundred-ton three-master, bound for the Bonin Islands south of Japan and the sealing-grounds of the Northwest Pacific" for a period of seven months.[4] This voyage provided the inspiration for his classic seafaring tale of a fur sealing voyage, *The Sea Wolf.*

Ms. Kienast's inspiration and main source for her early interest in Lewis Coolidge and his journal was Coolidge's granddaughter and my great-aunt, Eleanor Coolidge, who was well known to many around Peoria, Illinois, as "Aunt Nell." That was the affectionate name used under her photo in the bio piece in the *Peoria Journal Star* in 1942. A registered nurse, Aunt Nell was superintendent of Proctor Hospital in Peoria and the first superintendent of the Proctor Endowment Home and the Buehler Home in Peoria. The *Peoria Journal Star* piece notes that while growing up "on the Coolidge farm near Brimfield, one of the bright spots of her childhood were the tales her grandfather Lewis Coolidge used to tell her of his early adventures in sailing around Cape Horn, being held as a hostage by Spaniards and of the daily happenings aboard a sealing expedition . . . he also could quote Shakespeare by the hour." On her death in 1952, as specified in her instructions, Aunt Nell was buried next to her grandfather Lewis Coolidge on the grounds of Jubilee College near Peoria rather than in nearby French Creek Cemetery where her parents were laid to rest.

The adventures that Aunt Nell heard first hand thrilled succeeding generations of Lewis Coolidge's descendants as they read of them in an early transcription of his journal compiled by Charles McDonald of Elmwood, Illinois, in 1935. However, Evabeth Miller Kienast went back to the original journal for her transcription, which was completed in 1942. Austin Vincent Felt, a descendant of Lewis Coolidge through Coolidge's granddaughter Nancy Adelaide Coolidge Felt, oversaw the donation of the original journal to the Chase Special Collections of the Cullom-Davis Library of Bradley University in Peoria, Illinois, where it is well maintained and available to the public. Felt also was the transcriber for the 1843 letter from Lewis Coolidge to his nephew, included in appendix B. The Felt family has also donated the original of that letter to the Chase Special Collections.

JOHN PHILLIP FELT
Alexandria, Virginia, 2005

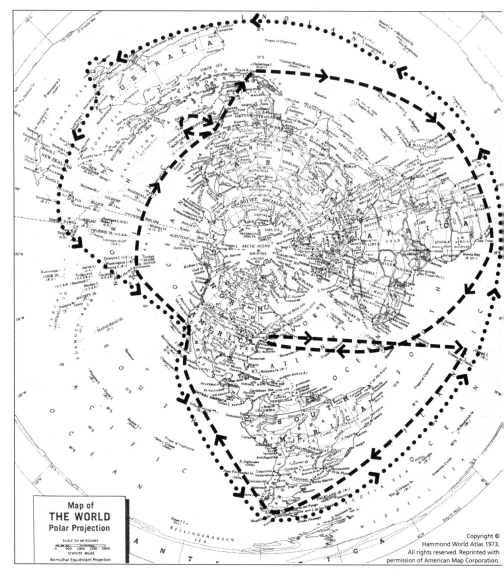

Map of the voyage of 1806–1811. Coolidge remained on the San Benito Islands and environs while the *Amethyst* returned to Gough Island, then almost to Australia, then back to San Benito.

LEGEND

— Ship's route with Lewis Coolidge aboard

== Ship's route without Lewis Coolidge aboard

Itinerary of the *Amethyst*

September 17, 1806	Departure from the Port of Boston
October 18, 1806	St. Nicholas Island
October 21, 1806	St. Iago Island
November 6, 1806	Crossed Equator
November 15, 1806	Trinidada Island
November 24, 1806–December 5, 1806	Goughs Island (left party to get seal skins)
December 24, 1806	45.11 S, 43.24 W
December 25, 1806	47.35 S, 51.39 W
January 13, 1807	Sighted Cape Horn bearing NNW 7 Leagues (21 miles) (12,900 miles from Boston)
January 17, 1807	59.48 S
January 20, 1807	Entrance to Straits of Magellan (Cape Villare)
January 27, 1807	Passed Cape Villare
January 31, 1807–February 15, 1807	Unnamed harbor on Coast of Patagonia (41.12 S, 74 W)
February 22, 1807	Island of Juan Fernandes sighted
March 3, 1807	14.39 S, 87.7.45 W
March 14, 1807	Crossed Equator at 99.56 W
March 17, 1807	3.49 N
March 19, 1807	5.23 N, 103 W
April 14, 1807	26.54 N, 126.24 W
April 20, 1807–May 1, 1807	Island of Guadaloup (29.5 N, 117.55 W)
May 1, 1807	left party to get seal skins
May 5, 1807	Island of Natividad (27.47 N, 115 W)

May 6, 1807–May 11, 1807
        Island of Cerros

May 16, 1807   San Benitos Islands

May 19, 1807   Guardaloup, left sealing party, return to St. Benitos

June 22, 1807   Amethyst departs St. Benitos to return to Goughs Island to pick up sealing party. Left at least two sealing parties on St. Benitos Islands, one headed by Lewis Coolidge.

June 22, 1807   Lewis Coolidge on St. Benitos, Cerros

May 16, 1808   Natividad, Guadaloup using small boat to sail from one to another.

May 16, 1808   Amethyst returns from Gough Island. Also had stops at St. Vare, Port Jackson, Norfolk Island, and Friendly Islands.

May 16, 1808–August 30, 1808
        In St. Benitos/Cerros/Guadaloup, collecting and processing sealing teams' pelts.

August 30, 1808   Final Departure from Guadaloup

September 20, 1808   Island of St. Rosalie (37.4 N, 10 leagues from main continent) one of present-day Farallon Islands off San Francisco, California.

September 24, 1808   Island of St. Barbara (33.25 N) in sight of St. Catalina.

September 24, 1808–September 29, 1808
        Bay of All Saints (Todos Santos) on the California Coast.

September 29, 1808   Passed St. Clements (32.53 N)

October 7, 1808   23.58 N

October 23, 1808–October 29, 1808
        Woahoo [Oahu, Hawaii]

October 31, 1808   Island of Atooi

November 22, 1808   Passsed Island of Pean (19.59 N) in the Ladrone Islands

December 7, 1808   Passed Bashee Islands

December 8, 1808   Sighted Coast of China

December 11, 1808   Passed Macoa (Macao)

December 20, 1808–January 31, 1809
    Province of Pingasanon, Philippine Islands

February 2, 1809   Manila, Philippines

March 13, 1809   Amethyst, in lawsuit, temporarily sold to a Spaniard; renamed St. Fernando

March 15, 1809   St. Fernando (Amethyst) sailed for Macao

June 11, 1809   St. Fernando (Amethyst) returned to Manila from Macao

December 6, 1809   Lawsuit settled; Amethyst departs Manila for Palau Islands

December 16, 1809–December 20, 1809
    Island of Luconia, Philippine Islands for repairs.

January 26, 1810   Koror, Palau Islands for bêche-de-mer.

June 3, 1810   Depart for Macao.

June 29, 1810–July 18, 1810
    Macao

July 19, 1810   Canton, China

August 9, 1810   Amethyst sold on Aug. 3; crew stays on board.

August 9, 1810   Crew paid off and discharged. Lewis Coolidge takes lodging in Canton.

November 28, 1810   Depart Canton as member of crew of Chinese vessel, Brum, bound for New York.

December 10, 1810   Straits of Banca

December 19, 1810   Straits of Sunda and Tamarine Island

January 27, 1811   Sighted Coast of Africa

January 28, 1811   Sighted Cape St. Aguillas (Cape Agulhas, southern-most tip of African continent, southeast of Cape of Good Hope).

February 13, 1811   St. Helena

February 22, 1811   Island of Accension

March 1, 1811   Crossed Equator

April 3, 1811   Arrived New York City

Photograph and sample page of Lewis Coolidge's journal

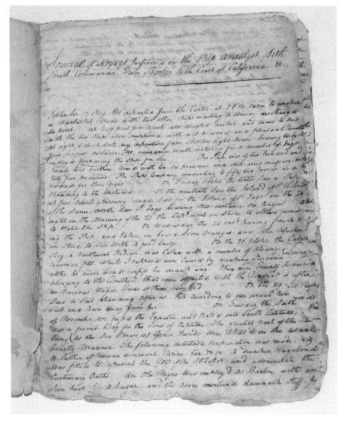

*Lewis Coolidge and
the Voyage of the* Amethyst

1806–1811

Permanent

N° 159. One hundred fifty nine.

In Pursuance of an Act of the Congress of the United States of America, entitled, " An Act _concerning the registering and recording of Ships or Vessels,_" John Dorr. of Boston in the State of Massachusetts

having taken or subscribed the oath required by the said act, and having sworn that he with Joseph Dorr, & Andrew C: Dorr of Boston aforesaid Ebenezer Dorr Jun? and William Dorr of Dorchester State aforesaid are the

only owners of the ship or vessel called the Amethyst. of Boston. whereof John Le Basquet. is at present master, and is a citizen of the **United States,** as he hath sworn.

and that the said ship or vessel was built at Salem State said in the year 1801. as appears by Register N° 55 issued at this Office March 22 1802 now cancelled, property partially transferred

And Thomas Melvill Surveyor

for this District ——— having certified that the said ship or vessel has two decks and three masts and that her length is Ninety five feet six inches. her breadth Twenty five feet, three inches. her depth, Twelve feet, seven & one half inches and that she measures Two hundred seventy & $\frac{11}{95}$. tons ;

No Galleries. that she is a square sterned Ship has and a figure. head ;

And the said John Dorr. having agreed to the description and admeasurement above specified, and sufficient security having been given according to the said act, the said Ship — has been duly registered at the port of Boston & Charlestown

Given under our **Hands** and **Seal** at the **Port** of Boston & Charlestown this Third Day of August in the Year one Thousand Eight Hundred and three.

Registration of the *Amethyst*. Photograph by J. Felt

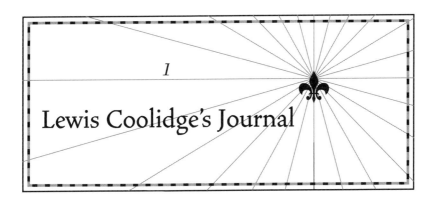

1

Lewis Coolidge's Journal

Journal of a Voyage perform'd on the Ship Amethyst.
Seth Smith, Commander.
From Boston, to the Coast of California. &c.—1806–1811
By Lewis Coolidge

September 17, 1806. We departed from the Castle,[1] at 5 P.M. Came to anchor in Nantasket Rhodes with two other Ships waiting a Wind. discharg'd the pilot. At half past five oclock A.M. weigh'd anchor, and came to sail with the two ships above mention'd with a S.W. wind and pleasant weather at eight o'clock took my departure from Boston lighthouse,[2] bearing W. by N. four leagues distance. No occurance worth noticing for a number of Days. imploy'd preparing the ship for Sea.

This Ship was of two hundred and Seventy tons burthen. Arm'd with ten six pounders, and other arms necessary with forty five Mariners. The Ships Company amounting to fifty two persons and provision'd for three Years.

On Friday October the tenth Saw a Ship standing to the Westward.

On the nineteenth Saw the Island of St. Nicholas[3] at five o'clock Morning. made Sail for the Island of St. Iago.[4] on the same month, 20 of the distance six leagues. saw St. Iago bearing N.W. distance six leagues.

At eight in the Morning of the 21 the Capt. went on Shore to obtain permission to Water the Ship.

On Wednesday the 24 ins't having finish Watering the Ship, and taken on board Some Oranges, and other refreshment. we stood to Sea With a good breeze.

On the 26 October, the Cabin Boy, a Northwest Indian, was taken with a number of Strange [word effaced here] uncommon fits, Which I suppos'd were Caus'd by drinking Mercuria altho, he never would confess he drank any. there were Twenty [illegible] belonging to the Amethyst, that were afflicted With the Venereal in Various Stages, Some of them very bad.

On the 29 [October] Saw a Sail standing after us, but according to our usual custom set Sail and ran away from her.

On Tuesday the Sixth [day] of November we cross'd the Equator, and pass'd into South Latitude. [This] was a jovial Day for the Sons of Neptune. The greatest part of the Crew being (as the Sea Phrase is) Green Hands, were shav'd in the usual beastly Manner. The following detestable preparation was made, Viz. a lather of human excrement, Wine, tar, &c &c. A drunken Vagabond was fitted to represent the GOD of the OCEAN, and administer the Custemary Oaths. An Old Negro was imploy'd as Barber, with an Iron hoop for a raizor, and the above mention'd damnable Stuff perfum'd the victims of this villainous conduct.

I was much'd suppris'd to See these inhuman measures Sanction'd by the Commander of the Ship and his two first officers. I saught for a reason to justify theese things, Which to me appear so highly ridiculous, but could find none that could such a scene supportable to a person, who has been us'd to regular life. however in a place like this, all Vanity is lost, and there is no new scene to charm the Mind or delight the eye. One continual sameness awaits our lying down and rising up, except a Gale of Wind to Enrage the Ocean and set us tossing on its surface, or Justice calls on the Commanders to inflict punishment on Some of the offending Crew.

I have often heard the Character of Seamen very much extoll'd.—but experience teaches me the Sad reverse—I am led to believe, that their Humanity does not reach further than their Sunday, viz, Five leagues at Sea. and I think it may justly be accounted for in this way. They are the most ignorant Class of People in Existance, and must remain So, having no mean for information. As Soon as they are off the Ocean, they are plung'd in intoxication, and vice, in the most dirty places in City's and Towns and among their own Class of beings. It is absolutely impossible that Brutal Ignorance should be a recepticle for refined Sentiments.

I have sometimes seen a ray of Sensibility break thro the dark Clouds which Confin'd it, but it was like the glimmering of a fire bug, in the dusky Evening, to the Splendour of the noonday Sun—

Saturday November 15. Saw the Island of Trinadada,[5] bearing S. by W. six leagues distance. Latitude 31 South longitude 25.35 West from Greenwich. [_____] Latitude 30 to Goughs Island, which lies in 40.15 South. we had [_____] gales from the Westward.

Friendship of Salem replica. The original was a three-masted, square-rigged,
342-ton vessel built by Enos Briggs of Salem in 1796–1797. Full-size replica
owned by the National Park Service of the U.S. Department of the Interior
and berthed at the Salem National Historical Site, Salem, Massachusetts.
The *Amethyst* also was a three-masted, square-rigged vessel built by Briggs.
The *Amethyst* was built in 1800–1801 and was smaller than the
Friendship, at 270 tons. Photograph by J. Felt

Thursday November 27 at 4 A.M. discover'd Goughs Island,[6] bearing E.S.E.
distance 6 leagues [_____] Seventy days from Boston.

At 9 oclock the Captain Went on [shor]e to determine the State of the Seal
on the Island, and the number [of] men necessary to leave to prosicute the
business of the Voyage. at Eleven [o]clock return'd, determin'd to leave Mr.
Dorr with nine Men.—Imploy'd landing provision, and Watering the Ship,
untill the fifth Day of December When we Saw, and lost sight of the Island, for
the last time lying in 40.15 South latitude, and 9.21 West from Greenwich. —

Goughs Islands has a most tremendous aspect from the Sea. The Mountains are prodigious high, and at this season were Cover'd With Snow, considerably below their Summits. the Whole Island is quite rocky, and barren, and
the Water's edge skirted with Precipices.

On the mountains are large pieces of stone resembling cinder, and Lava,
which I think is the same. which at some period isued from the boweles of the

Note on the construction of the *Amethyst* from Enos Briggs's account book.
Courtesy of the Peabody Essex Museum, Salem, Massachusetts

Earth.—From our departure from this Island untill the twenty-fourth day of December we had pleasant weather, interpers'd with some wind and rain.

On the twenty fourth, being in Latitude 45.11 S.and L. 43.24 West, there Came on a Tempest of Wind Snow, and Sleet. in its first onset we receiv'd a most furious shock which broke upon our larboard quarter, where it Stove in the quarterboards. the Sea making a clear breach over the ships deck. our rigging too suffer'd extremly, from the blow. amongst the rest, one of the Swiftures[7] Parted, and We were (notwithstanding the violence of the Wether) oblig'd to rig preventer shrouds[8] to Save the mast. At Midnight, We handed[9] every Sail, and scud before the Wind under the bare Poles, untill the 26, when the storm abated, & we made Sail, under our Courses, only, the Ship rolling gunne[l] too, made it impossible to carry more, in this Tempest. the Ship drifted[10] two and an half Knots (or miles) from N. W. to S.E.—On Saturday the twenty-Seventh cam on a heavy Gale accompanied with Snow and rain. At 6 o'clock A.M. hove too under the Storm staysail, making a drift of 2 miles pr hour N. by E. lat. 47.30 Long. 51.39 West.

The Tempest Continued from the 27 to the 29. With a high labouring Sea, Shipping large quantities of Wate[r] on deck.—

On Tuesday January 6, 1807, Capt. Smith finding o[f] means for governing William Green inefectual, was determin'd to receive no more insults and abuse from Him, and after consulting his officers, gave him a flogging with a small Rope prepar'd for that purpose.

The Cabin Boy Joe, receiv'd the Cat at the same time—according to the Sentance from the Inquisition—the Cat was known by Joe's Coat of Arm's—

January 13. At 11 oclock A.M. Saw (The Seat of Boreas) Cape Horn bearing N.N.W. distance Seven leagues. Cover'd with Snow and Ice. at the Same time Saw a large Ship standing in shore of us. At 2 P.M. the Wind increas'd to a hard Gale wh[ich] at 4 oblig'd us to lie too under the Storm Staysail[11] until 4 P.M. When the Ship Came bearing down upon us untill She was So near we cou'd discover her to be a man of war. We then made Sail the Ship "breasting the lofty Surge" and engulfing herself in the Deep which made it dangerous to be on deck. three of the most skillfull were lash'd to the Helm, and Cunn'd[12] by the Captain. At night We lost sight of the Ship—The Whole distance Sail'd since leaving Boston, untill we Saw Cape Horn, being 12,900 miles pr. log. On the 17 January We were in the highest South latitudes, viz. 59.48 in this latitude, it being the longest days. Daylight was not gone, but Was Sufficiently apparent to read on Deck, at any part of the twenty four hours. During our passage round the Cape, the Wind blew continually from the Westward, accompanied Wi[th] incessant squalls of Snow and Rain, which rendered the Weather very disagreeable.

On the 20. January Saw Land, Which Was at the entrance of the Streights of Magallan, know by the name of Cape Villare or Villaris. On the prospect of Villare I cannot but remark, that the Goughs Island had an aspect extreemly barren and desolate, yet this Island, or Cape, far surpasses it in the Wildness and horror of its appearance. It seeming to be entirely compos'd of inaccessible rocks, without the least mixture of earth or mould between them.—Theese rocks terminate in a vast number of ragged points which aspire to prodigious heigh and all of them Cover'd with eternal snow, the points themselves are on every side surrounded with frightful precipices and often overhang in a most astonishing manner, and the hills which bear them are generally Sepparated from each other by narrow clifts, which appear as if the Country had been frequently rent by earthquakes. for theese Chasms are nearly perpendicular, and extend through the Substance of the main rocks, almost to their very bottom, so that nothing can be imagin'd more Savage and gloomy than the whole aspect of this Coast.

There are large numbers of sea fowl in this latitude. We kill'd an Albatross, which measur'd from one extremity of the Wings to the Other, and found it to be ten feet 6 inches.

By reason of head Winds, which blew heavey, we did not weather away Cape Villare, untill the 27 January When the Wind Shifted, and we once more were able to proceed on our Voyage.

And now after all our solicitude, and the numerous dangers We had Pass'd in Coming round Cape Horn, We had great Consolation in the flattering hopes we entertain'd, that our fatigues were drawing to a period, and that we Shou'd soon arrive in a more hospitable Climate, Where We Should be repaid for all our Sufferings. With theese ideas We left Magallan, and Villar, with "storms and Tempests Settled on its brow" to experiance the celebrated tranquillity of the Pacific Ocean.

January 31. All hands imploy'd in Mounting Guns and making Catriges to be in readiness to enter a harbour on the Coast of Patagonia[13] to Wood and Water the Ship. Tuesday February 3. At 12 O' Clock, Noon, saw land bearing E.N.E. distance seven leagues, and Stood in for the Same.

At 5 P.M. Came to an Anchor in nine fathoms Water in a safe and Comodious harbour on the Coast of Patagonia Latitude 41.12. Longitude 74 We[st] being at the Southerly Part of the Eastern Side of the Island.

This Harbour abounds with Geese, Shags and a variety of other Sea birds. her[e] I went on Shore for the Second time Since leaving Boston, being out one Hundred and forty days.

All hands were employed in Wooding and Watering the Ship until the 10 February When having Completed our buisiness in this place at 4 O'Clock A.M. Weigh'd anchor to beat out of the Bay. but the Wind blowing a Gale, and it being thick and dark Weather, finding We cou'd not weather away the land, at Noon Wore Ship, and at 4 P.M. after Being out twelve hou[rs] regained the Harbour, and anchor'd on the Old Ground. We had scarcly furl'd the Sails before We Were oblig'd to let go both Anchors, the Wind being very violent— When going out of the Harbour, Mr. David Christie, who had lately been appointed fourth Mate of the Ship, was instantly Swept by a Swell of the Sea from the Sheet Anchor,[14] and went under the bows of the Ship—notwithstanding all possible serch being made—He Was Seen no more.—Peter Gellier, a Frenchman, and John Hollingsworth, at the eminent risk of their lives, Went in the Boat, to attempt his rescue.—;During the remainder of our stay here, all hands were imploy'd in their Several ocupations.

The mountains in the interior Country are Cover'd With snow considerably below their summits which I presume lies on continualy, this being the mid summer in South latitudes. Theese Mountains stretch from Mexico to the Streights of Magallan, and are Known by the name of the Cordillare[s.] the Islands, and Coasts of this part of Pategonia, are cover'd wi[th] Wood, and planted by the hand of Nature So thick, it is difficult to penetrate far into it.—

The Water is very good in this Harbour, and is a place very well fitted to Wood and Water Ships, that visit theese seas. Here are greens resembling potatoe tops, which the Captain made use of, and some small berrys, like Goosberrys. A Tree also grows here, the bark of which is as hot as Pepper. One of the men kill'd an animal in the Woods similar to a rackoon.—

February 15. the Wind Shifted to the South east. We joyfully embra[ced] the opportunity. Weigh'd anchor and proceeded to sea, with a fair wind being very much tired of a place where it hail'd, or rain'd, every day. The Whole Distance sail'd by log since leaving Boston being 15,366 Miles.—On Sunday February 22. Saw the Island of Juan Fernandez, bearing N by E. distance about ten leagues. at eight o'clock P.M. the Island bore the same, distance. three leagues, at 9 o'clock P.M. We were up with the small Island lying, and making the South West Point, call'd Goat Island.

We pass'd Juan Fernandez between the hours of ten and eleven oclock in the evening within two miles of the Lee Shore. The Wind blowing high from the Westward accompanied with freequent squalls of rain, rendered passing on this side dangerous.

This was the most interesting Night I ever witness'd. we were at one time so near the Shore, as to hear distinctly the noise of the Sea, breaking on the beach. and the horizon being overcast with flying, tempestuous Clouds. Cynthia,[15] my favourite Planet, seem to rush at intervals from behind their envious obscurity to observe our situation, and direct us the way "by the brightness of her Countenance."

Juan Fernandez is remarkable for being the residence of Alexander Selkirk, a Scotch-man, Whose life and adventours furnish'd D'Foe with the ground work, of that admirable Romance, Robinson Crusoe.—Tuesday, February 24. We took the South E. trade winds in latitude 30.30 our course being North 33.45 West. Long. 83.19, having Sail'd since We left Boston, 16,617 miles pr. log. variation 9.37. Eastily.

March 3. Longitude by Luna observation 87.7. 45 West from Greenwich. Latitude 14.39. South.

March 10. Caught three hundred Gallons Water and one Shark.

Saturday March 14th. pass'd from South into North Latitude, being from Gough's Island 100 days, and from Boston 178. Longitude 99.56. having Sail'd 18,745 miles. From three degrees of South Latitude, untill We cross'd the line, we had very heavy rain. March 17. Latitude 3.49 North. we had hard rain, lightning and thunder. March 19. light Winds, and calm. In crossing the line We had variable winds from three degrees of South latitude. This day we caught seven Turtles. it would naturally be suppos'd that this would be a great luxury to us. but the damn'd Scullion: they were intended to be made into soups, but prov'd nothing but a Vile unpalatable pernicious sophistication, balderdash'd

with a little Flour. which made a delatorious paste, in truth, it was so void of all
taste, nourishment and flavour, that a man might dine as comfortably (even
with out O.P.) upon a White frigasee of Kid skin gloves, or Chip hats from
Leghorn.—latitude 5.23 North. Longitude 103. West.

March 22. Caught a Shark.—"Come hither all Ye Epicurian Blades"—[16]

April 1. we took the NE trade Winds, in seven degrees North Latitude, but
found them much more variable than the South East trades. The NE trades
[which] we were crossing varied from East to North, but were generally from
N.E. to North.

April 14. Latitude by observation 26.54 North. Longitude, by taking the
distance of the Sun and Moon together with their respective altitudes, 126.24.

April 19. Saw the Island of Guardaloup, bearing E. by N. distance 12
leagues.

On the 20: civil time, at 7 o'clock A.M. the Captain Went on Shore. the Ship
stretching off, and on the land.—at 7 o'clock. Return'd, giving a favourable
account of the Seal.—

From April 20 to the 30, we were imploy'd in sirching the Island for water,
on the 29 day I set out to travel on the mountains, and thro deep glens an[d]
vallies in sirch of water, but could find none, that I thought might safely be
depended upon for the use of the men design'd to be left here.

After being gone three days, and Nights, having travel'd over most part of
the Island, I return'd to the Southerly part of it, where Mr Carr, and the remainder of the people, we[re] taking Seal.

The North part of the Island is cover'd with Ceder, and various kind of
bushes. the Land rises gradually from the Sea, to the midd[le] of the Island,
which is very high. the course of its ascent is often interupted b[y] vallies, and
hills of a peculiar Kind of red, and blue Earth. These Vallies wi[nd] irregularly
thro the Island, and the gradual swellings of the Hills, with their different
combinations of Colour, are most charmingly contrasted with the Woody summits of the Northern Mountains, rising in majestic Grandeur—The Cloud top't
peaks in the Center, which appear like a fantastic Vision—and the dark and
rocky promentories below.

There is the appearance in many places subtoranious fires, which probably
issued from the high mountains of the Island. Latitude 29.5 North. Longitude
117.55. West.

April 30 Peter Tinkham accidently a large bason, entirly of rock, containing
upwards of one hundred H[d][17] of Water. I never had an opportunity of visiting this remarkable Well, I cann[ot] discribe it particularly. no Kind of spring,
as could be perceived, led into it. t[he] water is not clear, of a white colour, as

if Chalk had been mix't with it, but. was different in taste, than any other. this fortunate discovery has saved immense troub[le] as the Ship wou'd inevitably have been obliged to go up the Coast of New Albion[18] for water, for the use of the men to be left here.

One great inconveniance atte[nds] this. the Water here is nearly four miles from the beach, Where the huts are erected. [Con]sequently the men will be obliged to bring it down over rocks, and thro defiles, [hard]ly passable, expos'd to "all Weathers," in Kegs of seven Gallons, made for the purpose. I am apprehensive this will create a difficulty among them, but to return.

After landing Mr. Carr, the first officer, and nine men, with provisions for the present, We proceeded on the first of May in sirch of other Is[land]s we being becalm'd under the high lands of Guadeloupe, we did not loose sight of land, untill May 3.

May 4. at four o'clock P.M. Saw land bearing from N.N.W. to E.N.E. distance seventeen leagues, and stood in for the same.

The Captain went to examine the Shore, but finding no fur seal, as he expected, ret[urn'd] to the Ship and beat to the northward. Latitude by Observation 27.37. North.—May 5. in the morning, saw two Islands, to the northward. plying to windwa[rd] for the same, we ran between the small Island of Natividad and the west poi[nt] of Saint Banca[19] on the Main Continent of America, and found in some places only seven fathoms water, rocky bottom, with large quantities of kelp and coral weed.

sent the boat on Natividad, and found large number of hair Seal, but cou'd see no Fur seal, as we expected.

This Island lie[s] in Latitude 27.47. north longitude 115. West.

May 6, 1807. At 6 o'clock P.M. the Captain went on Shore on the Island of Cerros[20] distance about ten mi[les] from Natividad. returned and Anchored in seventeen fathoms, sandy bottom the south east part the Island.

May 7. weigh'd Anchor and sa[il'd] up the Eastside of the Island, to water, and came to anchor in 28.3. nort[h] latitude eastily of the High Peak.—

Near the watering place, we found a number of Huts, containing some Cloathing, otter, fur seal and other Skins, which we concluded, by the Appearance in which they were left, had been abandon'd by Indians, who had been living on this Island, as we found Bows, arrows, and other implements of war, with some cloaks, and shoes, trim'd in the Indian manner. The Huts were made of skins, in a Conical form, and very small—we suppos'd that the Spaniards, who inhabit the neighbouring Coast of California, had taken the Indians from their habitations on Cerros. prepossess'd with this idea, We took some Skins and other Articles, that we thought might be most useful to us.—

May 11. A Mr. Woodward came on board in an Indian Canoe. with two Indians. He inform'd that He had been left on this Island by Cap. Windship of the Ship, *O'Cain* of Boston, with a number of Indians, for the purpose of collecting otter skins. That they then liv'd about ten miles to the Northward, in a place more secure from the Spaniards that inhabit the Coast and of Whom they felt some degree of fear. That the *O'Cain* had Sail'd to the Northward, where Captain Windship had about seventy Canoes, collecting Otter Skins, on the Coast of New Albion.

Captain Smith after hearing this statement, order'd every thing taken from the Huts, to be return'd, which was accordingly done, and dismis'd Woodward, with some presents very much to his Satisfaction.—Having finish'd. Watering the Ship, weigh'd Anchor, and proceeded to the St. Benitos, presents three small Islands, lying Twenty five miles, West of Cerros.

Saturday May 16. Came to an anchor, in nineteen fathoms water, rocky bottom, in the range of the White Rock, bearing W. by N. distance one half Mile. The extremity of the Isle's bearing NE./4 North, we were agreeably suppris'd to observe vast numbers of Fur Seal, upon the beach.—After landing provisions, and Water, the Ship on the 19, return'd to Guardaloupe leaving Thompson Patching, second officer, as President, and thirteen men, who began to build their Huts, and make preparation, to prosicute the business of the Voyage. Friday June 4, at civil time, at 6 o'clock P.M. the Ship came back from Guadaloup having left Mr. Carr, fourteen men.

June 14. The Ship went to the Easterly part of Cerros to water, leaving a number of men on the Benitos. the long boat, which had been deck'd, lengthen'd, and rigg'd as a Shallop with two masts, Sail'd the same time. this Shallop is intended to transport Water from Cerros to theese Isles. she is made capable of carying fourteen barrells at a time.

Captain Windship having return'd from the main, Captain Smith made a Contract with him, for five Sandwich Island Indians, to assist us in collecting Seal Skins.

June 22. The Ship having water'd, sail'd on her Voyage, back to Goughs Island, to take off Mr. Dorr & Company. I remain'd on the Three Sisters, (nam'd from its three Mountains) one of the Benitos, as Governor, with five men.

Stephen Howe with five men, proceeded by order of Capt. Smith, to the Island of Cerros to collect Skins there.

Whole distance, the Ship sail'd While I was on her was 22,582 miles, When I left her at the Saint Benitos.

St. Benitos Islands

––––––––––––––

Theese Islands present such scenery as CHATTERTON[21] wou'd have delighted to contemplate.

"Rock's pill'd on Rocks, as if by magic spell,
 HERE, scorch'd by Lightnings—There with ivy green"—

I have often paus'd to behold theese stupendous scenes, while seated on some wild cliff, where only the Moss cou'd flourish, and look into some glen, (where human feet never wander'd.)—so deep that the noise of the Sea, which broke violently on the beach.—was scarcely heard to mur[mur]

Over theese crags rise others of prodigious height, and fantastic shape.—some shooting into Cone's—others impending far over their base, in huge pieces of rock's, allong whose ridges was often seen others that, trembling even to the vibration of a sound, threatned to bear distraction in its course below.

Around on every side, far as the eye can penetrate, are se[en] only forms of grandeur.—The long perspective of mountain tops, tinged with Eth[er] blue, or peeping above the Clouds.—sombre Vallies, and peaked promentories, 'aford such a view, that REUBENS[22] wou'd have chosen for his canvas. I cannot express the sublime emotions, they often inspired.

The deep silence of theese solitudes are broken only by the scream of the Sea birds, flying from Cliff to Cliff, and the noise of the Sea, which breaks with awful violence on the beach.

The Island of Cerros, distance about five leagues, is seen very distincly in a clear day. the highest peak, by an observation, taken by Capt. Smith with the. Quadrant, is 4200 feet above the Surface of the Sea.

From theese Islands, I have often seen long billows of vapor Rolling—now excluding—and now opening, and partially revealing features, afording a Scene charmingly romantick.—My hut was so situated as to command an extensive view, of theese. (to me) inchanting pictures, the lovely and Sublime, of "Beauty sleeping in the lap of horror"[23] I felt comparatably happy—resign'd—and contented, and involuntarily exclaim'd with Thompson,[24]

> I care not Fortune! What you me deny,
> You cannot rob me of free nature's grace.
> You cannot shut the window's of the sky,
> Thro' which Aurora, shows her brightning face.
> You cannot bar my constant feet to trace
> The woods, and lawn's, by living stream at Eve,
> Let Health my nerves and finer fibres brace,

And I their toys to the great Children leave—
Of Fancy, reason, virtue, nought can me bereave

July 3 The Shallop sail'd for Cerros with Provisions &.c. leaving me with only one man, and Timothy Connor, who has been sick, the whole voyage, and who still continues unable to help himself. the immoderate use of Mercury has reduc'd him a Spectre.

A fur seal beachmaster. Drawing by Bristow Adams. "The Fur Seals and Fur-Seal Islands of the North Pacific Ocean," U.S. government report, 1898

July 28. one of the Whale boats, came up from Cerros, with five men who came up for their Chests, & they inform'd, that Patchen[25] had taken a boat at the Watering place, at Cerros, with five of Mr. Carrs Company, who embark'd in the Whale boat from Guadaloup, for the main Continent according to the account given of theese people it appears, That they made the Point of St. Banta, first at which place they left Henry Peck, who chose to take his road in the enter[ior] and has not yet been heard of. They then went upwards of one hundred miles allong Shore, Suffering very much from hunger, and thirst, living often. thr[ee] days without water, they Said, that their object was to go to Natividad, which lies about fifteen miles to the south end of Cerros, and there wait the arrival of the long boat, from the Benitos, having enter'd into an agreement with Helem the Carpenter, Alexander Walker, and others to take that boat, which then fitting to transport Water from Cerros.

After the Carpenter had finish'd A New head for the *O'Cain* and Captain Windship had given him his Pay, on the 30 July he went on to the Mountains of Cerros, and has not as Yet been heard off, but was seen by the Indians to get bread for _____ nights successivly. Alexander Walker, after two days absence, return'd [to] duty. The season being too early for sealing, there was no imployment, but improving our huts. Making Oil for our lamps, mogason's &c., fishing, catching young sea birds, and reading, was my principal imployment. My hut[26] was compos'd of rock, except the top which was of sea elephant skins, neatly sew'd togather when green. the door was a large flat stone, which I could remove at pleasure, my furniture consisted of a stone table, about two feet square, which projected from the Side of the rock, which made the inclosure. on this table, stood a lamp, a tin pot, two large muscle shells for spoons, and a jug of "Honest Water,"[27] cold as ice. my seats was two joints of the back bone of a Whale. my bed was placed in a small vacancy at the back part, principally of skins, a blanket, and a Sandwich Island Matt.

in the aperture's of the rock were plated Shell's of a great variety, and from the roof, hung the intire skin off a Dog fish, stuff'd. this alwas shew'd Which way the Wind blew, as exact as the Compass. a few volumes of Shakspeare which were the only books I had, we plac'd in the highest niche of the Wall. so much for my Hermitage.—

August 11. The Shallop arriv'd from Cerros, with thirteen barrels Water, out three days, she proves a bad Sailor, not keeping the Wind, to any advantage, and very leaky.

August 18. the Shallop Sailed for Cerros with. provisions.—Tim Connor very Sick.

August the 24. 'the Shallop arrived with Water. 2 days out. She brought two Indians. from this time to the 4. September, imploy'd in making a Smoke house, and a Seal Skin Canoe, which draws only four inches Water. Wou'd land thro the highest Surf.

[September] 5. Went round the largest Island in the Canoe with a handkercheif for a Sail. young Seal quite plenty all along Shore, to the Westward Saw a number of otter's. on returning was upset in the Surf Off the Northern Reef, owing to getting the Canoe broadside to the Sea, but got on Shore, with the Canoe, which Was damaged considerably. thinking there was too much danger in adventuring out with it again, and being afraid I shou'd be induc'd to, I cut it to peices.—; [it is obvious that Lewis Coolidge meant to write September for this second month, which he continued to call August]

[September] 14. Caleb Whitman taken very sick, vialent pains in his breast, gave him Elexir Salutes, and Castor oil, at Night 40 drops Laudanum, and increas'd the dose to 60, at Midnight, which had no sorifick effect, but producing insanity, and violent fever.

[September] 16. [Here it is obvious that Lewis Coolidge meant to write September for this second month which he absently continues to call August.] William Fo[rd] confin'd with the Scurvey in his leg. Whitman and Tim very sick.—the people begi[n] to murmur and grow refractory, have form'd* themselves into a Cabal, obey no order and swear they will leave the Island.

[September] 20. Whitman, continues very sick, as Also Tim and Ford.

[September] 25. the Shallop arrived from Cerros, with Water 4 days out. Patchen inform'd that Peter Richardson, and one Indian were sick on Cerros. Whitman on the threshold of Eternity.—On the 27 September, Caleb Whitman Died, two others remained dangerously Sick.

Oct. 1. The Shallop Sailed for Cerros, with Patchen, one boy, and three Indians. William Ford and all the Banditti taking Advantage of his Absence, left the Island in the twilight after taking nearly the Whole of Patching's Cloathing, and a number articles belonging to the Ship. they also took all Patchings Tobacco, A Pistol, with amunition, with which they Swore, they would kill the first one that intercepted them—They intended to make the point of St. Banca, on the main Continent, which lies about 14 leagues to the N.E. of this Island, and thence travel into the interior in sirch of inhabitants, and by Some mean get a Passage home.

They left me With Timothy Conner, who still continued unable to help himself, and one Indian.

By this damn'd Conduct, I was deprived of a boat to go to Cerros, if any misfortune should have hapned to Patchen.

On the 7. October the long boat arriv'd from Cerros, being out four days. two more Indians came up. we had now Water Sufficient to last six months. hauled the boat off the rocks, and dismantled [her]—

October the 10. A whale boat arrived from Cerros, with four men who informed that Howe, Peter Richardson, and one Indian was very sick. in the Evening I put up a few medicine intending to go down to Cerros the next day— The Medicine box, which was put on Shore for the use of twenty men, for fourteen months, was more like the draw of an old Woman's cupboard, compos'd principally of ointments, salve, rags, &c.

Oct—arrived at Cerros. found Peter hastening to "that bourne where no traveler returns,"[28] and Howe very lame but not otherwise indispos'd, the Indian boy dangerously sick, all affected, apparantly with the Scurvey.—

I was greatly pleas'd to find all the Huts, remarkably neat, and Clean, and the place selected by Howe, for his residence, exactly suited my taste. It was a deep valley, about three rods from the beach. the sides consisted of rocks and precipices. upwards of one hundred feet in heigt, and inaccessible. A few dwarf spruce trees, grew near the huts, and the weeping ivy, often threw its pendent foliage over the Steeps above, where the scanty Soil scarcely conceal'd their roots, and Where the light leaves, wav'd to every breeze, that flutter'd from the Ocean.

The silence of this melancholy spot is only interupted by the noise of the Sea, which (this being the windward Part [of] the Island) often breaks with awful violence upon the beach, or the screams of the Sea birds, which are Seen towering round the butting Cliffs.

October 16. Howe and Peter was put, as high as, the Waiste in the ground, but it being of a very light, dusty nature, it will do no good. the legs appear very much discolour'd, the toung, and gum's very sore, with a bad breath, nausia, and very low spirits, which are I think, evident marks of the scurvey.—William Wade Shott a deer.—

on the 20. October Howe and Peter confin'd themselves to their beds. notwithstanding, every exertion was made 'to persuade them from it. Went to the Eastward, saw a Grave about one half mile from the watering place, with a painted board at the head of it, with this incription, "Here lies the body of Captain Isaac Duck, late of the Ship *Porto Prince*, died at this Island, Oct. 1 1806, Aged 49 years."

Oct 27 Peter Tinkham and John Downs, taken with the Scurvey. Oct. 28. G.M. Bartlett, and Charles was taken with the Scurvey. Tom, the Indian getting worse. all the nourishment aforded them is a little flour and water no tea, or Coffee—or any medicine.

November 3. this morning the Indian boy died. The Poor Indian Atooi nearly 60 year's of age came into our hut in the morning for a light, about 3 o'clock. on his return he found the boy dead. [at] this he began to howl, according to the customs of his Country, and continued untill morning, making the most hidious noise I ever heard.

in the morning he rapt 'the corpse in a matt, in a sitting posture, binding it with strong Cords, but leaving the head uncover'd.

previous to its being caried out of the Hut, he knock'd out two of the teeth, and cut off a lock of hair, as a memento to its relations at the Sandwich Islands. It was with difficulty we found a place to bury the corpse, the soil being so hard and rocky as to be most impenetrable to a pick ax. we were also at a great loss for tools for this purpose, having nothing but an iron bar, a big shovell, and two wooden ones, besides having but three hands to work. it wasn't until five o'clock in the Afternoon, that we were able to dig more than 3½ feet. having Plac'd the Corpse on a Skin, we put a wooden pin thro each corner to ho[ld] it by, the old Indian Atooi leading the Way, and singing in the Sandwich Island Custom. the hoorid Yells that he made reverbrated among the rocks like the roaring of Cerberus. in imagination, the Corpse seem to have awakne'd and to have thrust his head thro the envelope to find the cause of such a discord.

The Corpse being set upright in the grave, its head could not have been more than one foot from the top after being cover'd.

It was not without a deal of persuasion, that we got Atooi the Indian willing to cover the head with a Cap, which we brought for the purpose, before we fill'd up the grave.

To prevent the Deer, Birds, &c. from molesting it, We cover'd it intirly with stones.

November 4. Barsella Simonds unwell. all the sick 'bout the same except John Downs, who is very bad, having got sores come out over his whole body. from this time we that were well, was imploy'd in mending the huts, building Chimneys, the weather beginging to grow Cold and tempestous, cutting wood and preparing for Winter.

nothing particularly occured untill the 13 Nov. When Peter Tinkham and John Downs confin'd themselves to their beds, in the last Stages of the disease.

on the 15 November I went up to the St. Benitos, leaving the old Indian to take care of the sick.

Arriv'd at 10 in the evening, and here I found, one boy, and two Indians, just expiring, with the Scurvey. Timothy Connor was the Same as when I left him having put up a few of the best medicine we had, the next day departed, and arriv'd at Cerros in the Evening, found the sick no better.

November 18 Shott 2 Deers.

On the 23 Atooi the Indian was taken sick, had a number of strange, convulsive fits.

November 26. at midnight Peter Richardson died.

What is rather remarkable, the lamp (which always burn'd till Daylight) went out the same instant, and left us in total darkness.—his death had considerable effect on the people, except Howe, who bore his sickness with great patience, and resignation.

Only three of us could attend to Peter's interment which took us the whole day.

Among some of his papers I found a letter from a female friend, beseeching him not to go to Sea—presaging his death—and expressing a strong presentiment of never seeing him again.

He belong'd to Westford, Massachusetts, and I cou'd not help lamenting, that he shou'd be drawn from the innocence, and beauty of a Country retreat, to the corrupt and boisterous occupation of a sea faring life.—from social happiness, amids't the grand simplicity of nature, which probably He might now have enjoy'd—but from which, He had now taken—an eternal farewel—

On the 30 Howe began to [com]plain of pains in his breast. the discolourations had nearly left his legs, and his mouth was much better. the disease had apparently got into his stomach.

December. 2. Came on a very violent gale of wind which sent the Surf nearly up to the huts. to the northward the Sea made the most awful appearance, the Sea breaking Against the rock for upwards of 100 feet, which made an intire sheet of foam, all along Shore. At about 4 P.M. a large Part of loose earth fell from the bluff, which made the point of the landing place, with a tremendous crash. At about nine in the Evening, we felt the Shock of an Earthquake which lasted about Seven seconds. This storm was made horrid, by the frequent glare of lightning, which heightned the effect of the scenery as it threw its red gleams, upon the Rocks, and Shrubery, leaving heavey masses of shade and regions of obscurity, which the eye fear'd to penetrate.

At about 3 o'clock the next day the Storm intirly ceas'd, and the deep repose of the Scene was undisturb'd by any Sound, but the low distant murmer of the Surf, which might be said to Soothe rather than interupt the Silence.

On the 5 December. a great alteration appeared in Howe, who being sensible of his situation, deliver'd me a number of Paper's to be deliver'd [to] his whife in Boston. Appear'd perfectly compos'd, and resign'd said he was quite willing to die, that he had no desire to live in a World, Which had for some Years back, been to him as a Sterile desert, that the pretended friendship, and duplicity of some, had been his ruin, and had left him to die in this obscure corner of the World.

I never left his bed side untill Thursday the 6, when He departed for that unknown World, leaving us "without a pilot, and without a guide"[29]

It is impossible to form the least idea of this melancholy moment. all the sick who, were able to go to the hut, stood arround the bed with hollow cheeks, and sunken eyes, witnessing the exit of one whom they all esteem'd as a friend, and of whom they expected Shortly to follow.

never while I live shall I forget this day and the following mighty tears, and sighs, Presentiments of sickness, and death fill'd every moment of the time. the gloom of the Season too, it being Winter, the mournful sighing of the wind, as it swept thro the Vallie, and its softer wispers among the Cliffs, was in perfect unison with our feelings, which were melancholy and cheerles in the extreme.—

Stephen Howe was a nat[ive] of Amherst, New Hampshire, and within theese three years, an inhabitant of Boston doing business under the firm of Howe & Wilder, in the English goods line. in the year 1804, He married Miss Caroline Goldsbury, a lovely girl of 16 years, daughter of Sam G. the whole family were pleas'd with this connection, except the father, who like another Sciotts,[30] treated them with great indiferance. Somtime in 1805, Mess. G.B. & Co. applied to H. & W. to endorse two notes of the amount of eight thousand, three hundred dollars, Payable to B.T.W.—under a consideration of Friendship. the notes were indors'd by H.& W. and were lodg'd in the Union Bank for Collection.

A little time after the n[otes] became due, Messrs. H & W receiv'd a Notification from the Bank, requesting payment, as the notes still remain'd in the Bank.

Dishonour'd by the promis[ors.] Under thees circumstances, as they cou'd not possibly collect Sufficient funds to redeem the Notes, they were under the hard necessity of closing their doors, and having the Whole of their property confiscated.

Howe applied to Mr. P.N. near the Union Bank, his old imployer, and I believe his fellow townsman, Who had before, promis'd to assist him in any exigency, but who now refus'd ungratfully to have any Concern in the affair, but in a few days after imploy'd Wilder to transact his business at Bordeaux. in about three Weeks he embark'd leaving his partner Howe, to stand the Brunt of this infernal buisiness.

This most villianous Deception is disgraceful to P.N. and stamps an indelible mark upon Wilder as an insin[cere] friend and a real Protius.[31]

Oh Friendship thou fond soother of the human breast,
To thee We fly in every calamity—
To Thee, we seek for sucour.—
To Thee the Case tir'd son of misery fondly retires.-
From Thy kind assistance, the unfortunate always hope
For relief.—
but may be ever sure of finding [dis]appointment."[32]

Soon after this disagreable affair, Howe remov'd to Amherst, where He Kept a School, which just aforded a pittance—[to] Keep him above Water—leaving his Young Whife Who 'Was then pregn[ant] at Charlestown, being unable to maintain her.

He has told [me] that She applid to her own home for assistance, but was inhumanly turn'd from the door by her Father, who preemtorily refus'd to do any thing for her, she being then six months gone with Child. Can there be a heaven and no Revenge!

Mrs Howe retired to Charlestown, depending on a Mere acquaintance for support, but who kept a small Shop in which Mrs H. assisted in tending, untill delicacy prevented her being in Public.

She was deliv'd of a Son in May, Which came into the World, without a friend to introduce it, but which—perhaps fortunatly—died in three Weeks after.—

In August, Howe saw Captain Smiths advertisment for Men Wanted for the *Amethyst* on a Sealing Voyage. he adress'd a letter to Capt S. in Which he desired to go as clerk or Steward, in Which last capacity, he was excepted.

His Whife, previous to the Ship's leaving Boston, took Passage for Halifax, in consiquence of an invitation from her brother, who is in very good circumstances.

In a letter to his Whife, dated July 1806, Howe observes, "If there is not a Change in the Conduct of some persons in Boston, I shall take means to end my anxiety in the Shortest way—Which you Will be convinc'd of in a Short time"

Alas his Words are too truly verified, for he now Sleeps in the Cold Grave, on the desert island of Cerros, in the most obscure corner of the World. Seldom press'd by human feet, "without a Stone to mark the spot"[33] but as the whole Earth is the sepulchre of virtuous men, his worth and Character will live in the breast of <u>fond rememberance,</u> and will survive marble monuments or local incriptions.

"O'er Him, whose doom The Virtues grieve, Aerial form's, shall, sit at Eve, And bend the pensive head."[34]

On the 11. December, Atooi the Indian's fitt's were more frequent, and he was in a state of insanity, untill the 17, when we found him lying on the ground in his Hut. it is suppos'd that he Attempted to come out—but fell—never to rise again.—4 others remain'd dangerously sick.

On the 28 Saw two sail, suppos'd to be Spaniards, endeavouring to Weather the Island of Natividad. at Noon they stood away to the Southward. having heard nothing from the Benitos since the 15 November, I felt anxious and the men appearing to be getting better, on the 29. I set Sail, and arriv'd in the Evening, and here I found that the two Indians, that I left sick with the scurvey the 15. Nov. had died. Tim Connor and the boy Was on the recovery.—and now it being most Sealing time, Patchen Went to Cerros, and brought the men to the Benitos, intending to begin here first—the Sick now began to gain ground every day, and here it will not be amis to describe this horrid disease. The common Appearances of the Scurvey, are large discolour'd Spots, dispers'd over the whole body, swell'd legs, putrid gums, and above all, an extraordinary lasitude of the Whole body, especially after any exercise, however inconsiderable, and this lasitude, at last degenerates, into a proness to swoon, or faint, on the least exertion of strength, or even the least motion.

The disease also is attended with a strange dejection of the Spirits, and with shiverings, tremblings, and a disposition to be seiz'd with the most dreadful terror's, on the slightest accident. Indeed it was most remarkable in all our, experiance of this malidy that whatever discourag'd the people, or at anytime damp'd their hopes, never fail'd to add new vigiour to the distemper, for it usually kill'd those who were in the last Stages of it, and confin'd them in their bed's. who were before [ca]pable of some kind of duty. So that it seem'd as if alacrity of mind and genuine thoughts were no [remainder here defaced]

On the 25 January, [1808,] The men being pretty well recover'd from the scurvey, We began sealing, Killing 402 the first day. We continued sealing untill the 29 February, having taken about 8500 skins, on theese Islands. on the 1 March prepar'd for Cerros taring the Shallops bottom &c. on the 3 March having properly secured the Skins, left letters &c. We left theese Islands once more for Cerros.

Island of Cerros.

March 3 in the Evening arriv'd landed the provisions and anchor'd the boat off shore. on the 5. began sealing, and continued untill the 14, having taken about 3000. 15. March went to the Island of Natividad. this island is surrounded with shifting sand banks and Rocks under Water. the beaches are Cover'd with Sea Elephant[35] and hair Seal. a great number of Sea birds of every denomination continually seen round the Island. there is no Water on the Island, consequently not a Subject of the Vegitable Kingdom can be Seen— We kill'd a snake here with two tails, of about five feet in length.—how this reptile shou'd subsist without water is a mistery. After being on this Island ten days, detain'd by the Wind, departed for Cerros, with about 2500 eggs, and a number hair seal skins for mogasons. on the 30 March went upon an allowance of bread, at three buiscuit pr. Day.

April 8 Saw a Sail standing to the Southward. suppos'd it to be the *Amethyst.* April 9. no Sail in sight—the people repine, and are discourag'd, in not [see]ing the *Amethyst.* Which has been expected theese three Months. on the 5 May myself, with two others, Set off on an excursion round the Island, providing ourselves with a blanket, three Pair of Mogason's and provisions for three days. about 5 oclock in the Evening of the Same day, We came to a large Cavern on the Sea Shore. on the top of the Rock, was a large Cross, apparantly made of the Sparr's of a Ship. this we Suppos'd to have been plac'd here by the Spaniards. after prostrating ourselves before this symbol of Christianity, in the true spirit of the Crusades. went into the Cavern "resting our heads upon the rock till morn"[36]—

In the Morning, we persued our journey, allong a Wild rocky Shore, untill about two oclock. When We were impeeded by a Point of rocks, streatching into the Sea, and thereby preventing our getting round it. We were then under Necessity of asscending steep precipices, and rocks, to reach the upland which having reach'd the road decended into glens. confin'd by stupendous rocks, grey, and barren, except Where some Stragling Shrubs fring'd their summit or patches of meagre vegitation tinted their recesses. further on Was Seen lofty Cliffs, and Spiring Points of Rock, from Whence the blue Waves of the Sea was Seen rolling in all its magnificence.

"Dear Valley" being not far distant We hurri'd forward to arrive there for the Night, and it was quite late before we made the entrance.

Its Rocks, crown'd with ivey to the [text defaced] part silver'd by the rays of the Moon, form'd a Contrast (beautiful beyond imagination) to the deep shaddow that involv'd the opposite cliffs, whose fringed Sumits, only, were tipp'd with light. While the distant perspective of the Valley, Was lost in the Yellow mist of "Cynthia's beam."—

"On the first friendly Bank, we threw ourselves down"[37] untill the Morning, When We resum'd our route to the East Point of the Island, Which is about fifteen miles from the huts. the Scenes which we this day Pass'd, were as wild and romantick, as any we had yet observ'd, with this differance, that beauty, even now and then, soften'd the landscape into smiles.

sometimes the high Mountain in the middle of the Island excluded all the view beyond, at others it admitted some partial catches of the distant scenery, which gave hints to the imagination to picture landscapes more interesting, more impressive, than any that had been presented to the eye.—at about 12 we arriv'd at the Watering place. Where the Ship first anchored, and my fellow travellers, being anxious to get home, we persued our course allong a White Sandy beach, and arriv'd at the huts about nine o'clock.

I cou'd not repent having taken this fatiguing jaunt, tho we were frequently oblig'd to walk along the rugged precipice. and Climb the steep, and flinty Mountain. The wonderful Sublimity and Variety of the prospects, repaid me for all this, and the pleasure express'd by my Companions, heighen'd my own and, awaken'd all the delightful emotions which the Charms of Nature inspire.—

We now began to feel extremly anxious for the Arrival of the Ship, and scarcly a day Pass'd, without our ascending the Mountains, to "streach the eager eye"[38] in sirch of a Sail.

on the 9. of May Saw a Sail Standing to the Eastward, sent a man to the Watering place to Watch her Motions.

The next day saw (apparantly the Same) a Sail standing toward Natividad, 4 leagues distance, but soon. after She wore, and stood to the Eastward. on the 11 the Man return'd and inform'd, that the ship was call'd the *Triumph*,[39] belong'd to New Haven, and Was commanded by—Brintnall on a Sealing Voyage. She had touch'd at Guadaloup, and left a Clan. She anchor'd at the Watering place.

on the 12 Patchen went to the Eastward on a visit to Capt. Brintnall, arriv'd home the next day, and inform'd that our Men at Guadaloup Were all Well, and had taken about 15000 Seal, that Brintnalls men had taken upwards of 20000. Mr. Carr had given over the *Amethyst,* and had Partly Contracted with Capt. B. to take them off the Island.

On the 14 May Saw a Sail Standing to the Westward. Suppos'd to be the *Triumph* bound for the St. Benitos.

May 16. at 9 Oclock A.M. Saw a Sail to the Westward, standing for Cerros, after passing the bluff, She hoisted her Colours. three Gun's, and hoisted her boat out, Which convinc'd us, she Was the *Amethyst.* at 12 the boat landed at the Westward, being prevented by the surf, at our lan[ding] place, When we recognis'd Our old Shipmates to our great joy. All hands went to the Eastward in the Evening, Where the Ship join'd us.

The *Amethyst* arriv'd at Goughs Island in September, after a very boisterous Passage round Cape Horn. She found Dorr with his clan all Well, they having about 5000 Seal. After being at this Island twenty days, departed 'for St. Vare[40] where She took 300 Seal, from thence Sail'd for Port Jackson,[41] and arriv'd about the middle of December. after being at this place a few days went to Norfolk Island[42] to Wood and Water the Ship. from thence Sail'd for the Friendly Islands[43] for Refreshments. In March Sail'd for Guadaloup, and arriv'd the 12 instant. Left Mr. Dorr with nine Men, and proceeded to the St. Benitos Where [word is defaced] was left with Some hands, Who are now imploy'd in taking Skins. [All] hands Were imploy'd in Watering the Ship and overhauling her hold un[til] the 29 When We Sail'd for the St Benitos, leaving Cape Cod Jack with ten [on] Cerros.

On the 30 arriv'd at the St. Benitos, imploy'd in taking Seal. on the 5 June When the Ship return'd to Guadaloup, leaving Mr. Carr with men to collect Skins. We found the Ship *Triumph* lying at the Ben[itos]. on the 4 June. She Sail'd for Guadaloup leaving Seven men for the purpose of collecting Seal Skins.

On the 28 June, the Ship arriv'd from Guadaloup, being gone twenty four days.—

July 4. at Sun rise the Ship fir'd seventeen Guns, all hands with the *Triumph* people, din'd together on two roast pigs, two bushell muscles, four bushell pancakes, and one half pint of the Necter of New England [rum], which was. toss'd off with the following toast, from the President. Our Native Land, May She Continue to be Independant, While the Earth bears a plant, or the Sea, roll's its waves. Mr. Hubbard, of New Haven, belonging to the *Triumph*, a fine young fellow, then Sang "Hail Columbia" this was preceeded by a Reel, to the air of Yankee doodle, on the Violin, by the Cook of the *Triumph*.

Captain Smith, and Mr. Carr, dining together on board the Ship, it Was motion'd and Seconded, that the following be Sent to them.

At a Meeting of a few of the Sons of Neptune, belonging to the Ships *Amethyst* and *Triumph* on the fourth of July, it was unnanimously agre'd that Joseph Hubbard, Barsella Simonds, William Tisdale, and John Lennas, be a committe, to wait on their respected Commander, Seth Smith Jun. Esq. and Mr. Moses Carr, with the thanks of the Company, for their excellent good cheer, and request them to drink the following toast. The President of the United States of America, and also request the favour of their Company on Shore, at about five oclock to hear the Address of "Hanibal to his soldiers, previous to the battle of Pharsalia,"[44] to be spoken by Mr. Hubbard, from the Summit of a Rock.—

the paper was presented by Hubbard—his right arm being naked to the shoulder. the boat was row'd by four Indians, with half minute strokes.—the Committee were receiv'd on the quarter deck, and the following answer return'd.

"Captain Smith and Mr. Carrs compliments to the Company on Shore. will honour themselves by drinking their Toast, under a Salute of three Guns, which will be a signal for the Company on Shore to join in the toaste.—will also come on Shore"—

the boat then return'd on Shore, with one bucket N.E. which Was the principle, object. "Bachus now set spurs to his steed."[45]

Soon after the Captain and Mr. Carr came on Shore. the Captain was waited upon by Hubbard to the Chair of the president. an Indian stood near with two Glass, Which Were presented to Captain Smith, and the President, who rose, join'd glasses and drank the following sentiment. Familiarity bounded by decency—and friendship unbounded by interest. The Captain then took the Chair, and a number of airs were play'd upon the Violin, in good taste.—the, following toastes Were drank. By Captain Smith, "Our Whifes, and Sweethearts"—By Mr. Carr, "Success to all honest Seamen" By Hubbard, "The Fair of America, and a speedy passage to their Arms, the Haven of bliss"—By William Tisdale, "The State of Connecicut the most Federal in the Union"—By Myself, May diffident Merrit, be ever protected.—

At about five o'clock Hubbard deliver'd Hanibals, address. he was plac'd upon a high Rock, Which overlook'd the beach, Where the people Sat in Mute Attention. He was naked to the Waiste, except a black hankerchief tied round his Shoulder's. the lower part of his person, was conceal'd by the rocks. in his hand he held a sword. The effect Was striking, and the speech was Spoken excelantly well.—At Sunset the Ship fir'd three Guns—The dinner was excellent—the pigs were bak'd in the ground in the Sandwich Island manner—the Muscles made capital Soup—the Cakes were PANcakes indeed—and the Rum was equal to Jamaica—the people Were agreeable, and in their Senses—untill nine oclock P.M.—Thus pass'd the fourth of July on the Benito Islands.

We Continued sealing untill the 26 July. When having taken every thing off the Island, Weigh'd Anchor at 10 A.M. and came to Sail with the Wind at NW—arriv'd at the Island of Cerros, at about 6 P.M. found that Patchen had taken about two thousand Seal. All hands were imploy'd Sealing, and taking the Skins off the Island.

July 30 the ship sailed to the Estward to Water, leaving part of the hands taking seal at the Westward.

On the 3. August having finish'd Sealing, took every article off the Island, and on the 5, took our last adieu of theese Islands, taking our Course for Guadaloup.

August 11. Went on shore on the NW. part of the Continent: the land rises gradually from the Sea and the Shore is very rocky, being Most an entire Clift all along the Coast.—on the 13. pass'd the Benitos. Saw a Ship at Anchor, suppos'd to be the *Triumph.*

on the 22. Saw land bearing NW. 6 leagues dis-tance. at 2 P.M. the Captain went on Shore, return'd with a Number Sea birds and some hair seal Skins. August 24. Saw Guadaloup bearing W.S.W. distance five leagues.

At 6 P.M. got up with the North head but no boat coming off, stood to Sea. the next day, at 10 A.M. made the Island, and hoisted the boats out. Went on Shore, found that Dorr had gone to the South of the Island with all hands except two men who were sick. imploy'd taking off the Skins which amount to about twenty thousand.

On the 27. Joseph Stratton and Nathan Dearing left the Ship, and Went on to the mountains, leaving a letter, which mention'd their design of staying on the Island, and requesting the Captain to leave some provisions, a boat &c. All hands imploy'd in taking the Skins off, and preparing the Ship for sea. Mr. Dorr arriv'd from the Southward.

On the 29. Thomas Keith, Charles Abbey, John Downs left the Ship. They took about 600 bread, 1 barrell Pork, and a few other Articles, their object was to remain on the Island, and Seal on their own Account.

On the 30 Sail'd in Sirch of more Islands, near the Main Continent, taking our last leave of Guadaloup, lying in latitude 29.5 North, Longitude 117.55 West. Captain Smith left in one of the Vallies two Casks bread, 1 barrell Pork, some Medicine, and a few other articles, for the Men that Elop'd.[46]

| From Guadaloup to the Main Continent

September 6. 1808. The main mast Was found to be sprung very dangerously, a foot below the head. on the 13 Came on a very heavey gale of wind, and Continued blowing for four days, the land about Seventeen leagues to the Westward of us. soon danger Was apprehended, the main Mast being in a bad situation.

On the 16, after a Very boisterous Night, a Sail was discov'd about Seven miles astern of us, made all Sail possible and left her in a Short time. there being a number of Spanish vessels generally on this Coast, the Captain thought it prudent to make Sail from her.

At 12 O'clock the Same day it being very moderate, made the land, and Saw Smoke on Shore, suppos'd . to [be a] signal of invitation from the Indians.

The Mountains appeared very different from what we have seen on the Coast, being very thickly Wooded, land very fertile.

On the 20. The Captain went on Shore expecting to find fur Seal, at Noon return'd, having Seen no living Creature, except a few Sea birds. this Island is

Call'd St. Rosalie,[47] lies in latitude 37.4 North and is about ten leagues from the Main Continent.

September 24. At 12 P.M. made the Island of St. Barbara.[48] On coming in with the land Saw a Smoke, suppos'd to be made by Spaniards. At 2 P.M. the Captain Went on Shore with an extra number of men, Arm'd, with about 50 bread, Some Cotton Hankercheifs to trade for furs.

Saw a number of Creatures, male and female, in the Human form, intirly Naked. they Were painted in a variety of Colour's, and arm'd with large peices of bone. it was not without great perswasion, We prevail'd on them to come to us.

The FAIR greeted us with a—horrid grin.—The men frown'd upon us.

They wou'd not take the bread, or any thing, except two or three hanker-chiefs, for which they gave us a basket of onions.

They having no furs, or any kind of Refreshments, left them in a Short time, and Stood for St. Catalina[48] then in Sight, to the Northward.

St. Barbara lies in latitude 33.25. North.—on the 26 September Pass'd an Island not laid down in the Charts, made our course for the Main Land about seven leagues Distance.

At three o'clock came to an anchor in Seven fathoms Water in the Bay of all Saints. (Todos Santos)[50] on the Coast of old California. the Nearest point of land bearing NW. by N. three Miles, and the Above Island E½N. five leagues distance.

The boat went on Shore at the head of the bay, at four oclock return'd having seen a few Indians, but no otter Skins, as was expected, at Sun Rise the Next day, saw two horsemen coming down from the mountains. they made a Signal for us to come on Shore. The Captain sent the boat with Mr. Carr the Cheif officer, and Peter Tellier as interpriter.

The Spaniards inform'd, that they had come from the Village of Deaux Anges,[51] about thirty Miles in the interior, for a load of Salt, but having Seen the Ship, they had come to trade with us.

Mr. Carr contracted with them for Some bullocks, vegitables, and tobacco, the men agreeing to bring them in three days.

They Said that a number of their friends had otter skins at Deux Anges, which they Would be glad to dispose of.

27 September. a Canoe with two Indians came on board, with fish, Shells &c. gave them a few beads, iron hoops, nails which they were very Well pleas'd With. They were intirly Naked, except. a Small band of Woolen Stuff, roun'd the Premises.—

On the 28 I went on Shore at an Indian village. In one of their Huts, was the most horrid spectacle, I ever witness'd. This Was a Child, apparantly (from its size) about seven Years of age. A perfect Skeleton, the bones in some places showing above the Skin—the head without any hair, and the eye's gone, So that the intestines were visable Within—the Skin contracted round its features, and full of holes, like a honeycomb.—its mouth wide open, Showing the tounge, green and livid—its fragile form, just vibrated, on the confine of eternity—a convulsive start, or Spasm, at intervals, prov'd that it had life.—by What I could understand from the Indians, I conclud'd, that this poor child, was the Victim of Superstition.

The Child in its infancy, being Sickly, Was continually laid in the Sand, on the beach, expos'd to the burning Sun, the GOD of the Indian, depending on its rays, to revive it.

The mother appear'd to be fond of it, mourning over it, and nursing it with great tenderness—I Saw a number of Indians, intirly blind.

The Mother seeming to expect I would give her Something, and taking a fancy to My Check Shirt, I immediatly off with it, and thereby, blistered my skin to Such a degree, before I reach'd the boat, that I "groan'd in agony." This, togather with the horrid Object that I had Seen, so disconcerted Me, that I involuntarily exclaim'd "There is Not another World"—"Death is an Eternal Sleep"[52]—on the boats landing at this place, the Second time, The Child was lying in the Sand the Mother attending it.

On the 29 September. Saw a Man on horsback on the Upland, Making Signals, for us to come on Shore. Sent the boat immediatly and found him a Spaniard from Deux Anges, informing us of the Sailing of two Frigates, and a brig, in persuit of us, they having information of our being on the Coast.—This Spaniard was very desirous to trade with us, having five hundred Otter Skins at Deux Anges, but advis'd us to get under way directly as he expected they would be at Porto St. Pedro[53] by Sunset. Previous to our leaving the Shore, an Indian arriv'd on a Mule, With ten otter Skins, offering to trade. the Captain sent a few goods on shore, and gave the Indian, one piece India cotton, one Cloth Jacket and two hhkfs[54] for the skins.

The Spaniard was presented—with two hhkfs, Cost about twenty Cents, for his very important information!—

This Cavilero put me in mind of Gil Blas,[55] and Don Quixote.—he was about six feet high, about forty years of age, of an olive Complection, his Mustachoes curling up to his eyes, lean and muscular built. he Wore blue Cloth britches, unbotton'd at the Knee's, a belt around his Waist. Boots with the tops turn'd down, to the anckles the leathur not tan'd, and ornamented,[56] with a variety of impressions. a broad brim'd Hat, flop'd over his eyes. On mounting his Rosinante, which was a curious kind of shambling Jack "spavin'd and shoulder Shotten"[57] he bid us a thousand "Adieu Seignors" and Went off in a Crazey gallop.

This Spaniard whose name is Jesse Bartolemeo told me, that the Ships *O Cain, Derby,* and *Minerva,* had touch'd at Porto St. Pedro. the Captain of the last Ship Was indetted to him to the Amount of one hundred & forty Dollars. He requested me on my arrival home to call on David Green and Son, the owners of the Minerva, and desire them to examine into the affair, and remit him the Amount in blue Cloth, some fine linen, and other good articles.

Elijah Bronson and Timothy Conner being bad With the scurvey, it was thought advisable to bury them halfway in the ground, it being very excellent and rich. Asa Warden being Set on Shore to atten'd on 'em, took that opportunity to elope. The Wind breezing at 2 oclock, We weigh'd anchor and Stood to the Northward, with all Sail Set.

in the evening the Captain propos'd to all hands, to go in Sirch of more Islands for seal, reminding them of their ingagement to that effect, "to go untill a Voyage Was made." The Men objected, representing their distress'd situation for Want of Clothes, and urging the important necessity of getting refreshments, to extirpate the remains of the Scurvey Which Still afflicted Some of them, and the uncertainty of finding Seal &c.—after a little altercation, the Captain concluded to bear away for the Sandwich Islands on her Way to Canton. At 9 P.M. Pass'd the Island of St. Clements,[58] lat. 3.2.53.N. at 12. the Isle bore West, 9 leagues distance.

October 7. Struck the N.E. trade Winds, in latitude 23.58. our Course being S.W. theese Winds blew very steady, With little Variation, but producing a large hollow Sea, right aft of us, Which Made the Ship roll gunnel, too.

On the 21 October Made Oyhee,[59] bearing S.W. distance seven leagues, and the Island Mowee[60] bearing S.S.E. distance about fifteen leagues. Made all Sail for the Island of Warhoo.[61] At 10 oclock on the morning of the 22 Saw Malahi,[62] bearing W by S. distance 9 leagues. At Night stood off the land With Short tacks.

an the 23. Saw Wharhoo, bearing W.S.W. 10 leagues distance. At 12 P.M. Came to an Anchor in seven fathoms Water—

I shou'd fail were I to attempt to describe the enchanting beauty of theese Islands. Here it may truly be Said, that the simple productions of unassisted Nature, excites all the fictitious description of the most animated romance.

Woahoo may justly be call'd an Arcadia, and I doubt, but it may vie with Arcadia in every thing but Climate.—I am sure it excells it in Verdure, Wood, and Water. indeed this Country wou'd be a perfect Paradise, if it was not curs'd with a Weeping Climate, owing to its high Mountains, its northardly situation and expos'd to the Vapours of the Ocean.

The inhabitants are very stout athletic people, strait, and hansomly proportion'd, and their countenances are far from being disagreeable. The Women are Small and much lighter than the men, possessing great vivacity, and in my opinion a Considerable Share of beauty. their teeth in particular, are of the most brilliant Whitness, showing thro lips, that wou'd invite even Diogenes to press.

Their dress is very light, and very conveniant—for Children of Nature, having nothing but a kind of shawl, over the bosom, with a Small band, round the—premises—

They are very fond of the Whites, for in a little time after our Arrival, more than four hundred, came off in Canoes, with every Kind of fruit in abundance, and so eager were they to come on board, that numbers jump't overboard, and clim'd up the Ships side, and without any prelude, overwhelm us With Caresses.—the, men repaid the girls, by returning their embraces with greatest ardour, and being fresh, and strong, were Capable of doing justice to this heavenly Sex, who in this Part of the World, were not averse of bestowing their Caresses with redoubled transport. We cou'd now exclaim with Othelo,

> "If after every Tempest, come such calmness,
> Let the Winds blow, till they have Waken'd Death. and let the labouring bark, Climb hills of Seas Olympus high, and duck again as low as Hell's From Heaven—So THIS is all"—[63]

It is our connection with Women, that gives a proper bias to our inclinations, and by abating the ferocity of our passions, engages us to that gentleness of deportment, which we stile Humanity. The tenderness we have for them, softens the ruggedness of our own Nature, and the virtue's we put on to make the better figure in their eye's, Keep us in humour with ourselves.—

On the 29. having Wooded and Water'd the Ship and taken in refreshments, consisting of Goats, pigs, tarro, potatoes &c. with some Rum distill'd from the tea Root, and considerable fruit, We took leave of Woahoo, a place Which I shall ever remember, for the fondness of the Women, the generosity and urbanity of the Men and the delicacy and variety of its refreshments, which tended effectually in a short time to eradicate the remains of the Scurvey, which still remain'd among some, after the rest of the Company, tho indulging themselves without the least moderation were very healthy. We shou'd sometimes increase the motion of the machine, to unclog the Wheel of life, and now and then take a plunge amid the Waves of excess, in order to case harden the Constitution. A Change of Company is as necessary, as a Change of air, to

Promote a vigourous circulation of the Spirits, which is the very essence, and criterion of good health.—

October 31. Made the Island of Atooi.[64] At 10 A.M. the King, with a large retinue of Cheifs, Women &c. Came on board, with a number of pigs Goats, &c. as presents.

November the 1 at 9 o'clock A.M. Stood to Sea, with a fresh breeze, our Course being W by S. for Canton.

on the 3. November, after a very hot day the Moon was discover'd to be Eclips'd, begining about seven O'clock, and continuing totally obscur'd untill half past nine. The Evening was very mild with gentle airs, but a very high labouring Sea.

At 12 had a number of squalls, with lightning,—latitude 20.3 North. on the 11 By taking the distance of the sun and moon togather with their respective Altitudes, found our longitude was 102 ½ E.S.E. from Greenwich being in E. longitude.

on the 22. pass'd the Island of Pian,[65] bearing W.S.W. 15 leagues distance in latitude 19.59 N. over the Ladrone Islands.[66]

Dec. 6 at 4 P.M. Saw a Sail to the Northward, standing for us. at 5 She fired a gun and hoisted American Colours. Hove the Ship to at ½ past five, she came athwart our stern. When We found her to be the *Guatamosin* of Boston, William Granville Master from the North West Coast bound for Canton.

On the 7 pass'd the Bashee Islands.[67] imploy'd in putting the Ship in a posture of defence for passing the Ladrone Islands. at 10 P.M. Saw two Sail boats, suppos'd to be Ladrones[68]—on the 8 Dec. Saw Land, the Coast of China, bearing S. by W. eight leagues, and saw the *Guatamosin* lying to for us, it Was agreed by the two Captains to bear company thro the Linsa passage,[69] laid off and on, during the Night, With short tacks.

December the 9. At daylight made Sail, and follow'd the *Guatamosin* thro the Passage, with a good breeze. At about 11 oclock saw a large vessel curiously rigg'd, and ornamented with Colours, come out from the Shore, and make Sail for Us.

All hands were order'd to quarters, supposing it to be ladrone, we being about one mile and an half from her, and the *Guatamosin* about a Mile.

At about 1 P.M. it breez'd up, and we left her a'stern. At 3 a large boat came off from the Shore, and fought her about 3 glasses [duration of naval actions, one and one-half hours], with great violence. The Ladrone having her masts shot way, other got clear at this time. We were about 3 miles ahead of them, becalm'd under the Mountains. The Captain thought the large one to be a friend to the other, and meerly manouvering to entrap us.

At 5 We having no wind, She came up with us, with her sweeps.[70] All hands were prepar'd, on board, to sell their lives, as dearly as possible, each Man being Arm'd with two pistols, a sword, and boarding pike—the large guns were loaded up to the muzle, with grape and Canister.

on coming up With the *Guatamosin,* We were agreeable Suppris'd to See her let go the Anchor. Soon after Which the Captain, with Granvile, Came on board, When We understood, that She was a Chinese Junk, from the Phillipine Islands, bound for Macoa, and the one She engag'd was a Ladrone. The Chinese had five men Kill'd and several wounded. the Captain supplied them with some medicine.

Here we lied at Anchor, with springs upon our Cables, all Night, waiting With great impatience for the morning. Thro the night, We could see the Signals of the Ladrones, all along Shore.

on the 10 at Daylight we weigh'd Anchor and Stood for Macoa, about 15 leagues distance. All the Way thro this infernal Passage, We Were Surrounded by the ladrons[70] and were continually apprehensive of being attack'd by them. When we Should inevitably been sacrific'd, if the Wind Should fail us. the Mountains being Very high makes this often the Case, and the Ladrons who live Along Shore have their eyes upon every vessell that passes them.

11 December at 10 A.M. got thro the Passage, and here we receiv'd the News of war, between the English and Americans, by a Chinese boat, Who boarded the *Guatamosin,* the Captain of Which, immediatly rounded too and inform'd us of the event. both ships then "haul'd their Wind,"[71] to stand thro the Passage, to get to sea, but there being but little Wind, We were off the entrance, the Whole Day, without gaining a mile. At 2 P.M. Saw a large Ship with a Schooner in Company. We were now Certain of being taken, and all hands secur'd his little, as well as possible.—at 5 o'clock the Ship, Which Was about five miles from us, a 64, fired a Gun, and hoisted American Colours.

We waited Night With the greatest anxiety, and impatience, the Captain being determin'd, the wind then blowing fresh and fair, to run the Ship by the great Ladrone, in hopes of escaping—both our Ships Continued to beat untill Sunset, When We fire'd a Gun and hoisted our Colours.

We left the *Guatamosin* about seven Oclock, and ran before the Wind by the Great Ladrone, all Night, with a Stiff breeze. At about 11 Ran Past Macoa,[72] in not more than four fathoms Water, and could very plainly percieve the lights &c. on Shore—The following daily occurances, from My Journal, may convey Some idea of the anxiety of the Moment.

Dec. 12 Blowing Fresh. A Number of Sail in Sight, the Ships Course S½W for Manila. A Sharp lookout at the Fore & Main topmasts heads.

" 13 Still blowing heavey, but carying full, no
Sail in Sight. Some prospect of escaping. Wds. with heavy squalls.

" 14 Continues with squalls. At 11, in all Sail, Sprung the mizen top gallant
yard. at ½ past 11 Crowded full Canvas, looking out aloft pt. Watch and hel-
men, at eight P.M. Shortned Sail for the Night.

" 15 Came on With rain and violent squalls. Not more than three degrees
from the Island of Luconia, our course due E. looking out aloft.

" 16 Steady and fresh breezes. Set all Sail by the Wind. At 10 A.M. Rigg'd
preventer Shrouds upon the Mainmast. Our Course E.S.E. expect to make
Land by sunset—at 8 P.M. no land in Sight. Caried away the fore top sail haul-
yards. Wds squally.—

" 17 At 10 A.M. Came on a heavey Gale at W.N.W. Which oblig'd us to lie
too. at 3 P.M. the Gale increases. Sent down the top gallant Yards. at 5. Ship'd
a Sea which Caried Away all the bulwarks on the larboard side, stove the Camboose,[73] and did other damage. Thro the Night, blowing tremendously. and
the Sea Making a Clear breast over the Ships deck.—At 2 oclock, laid her too
under the Storm Staysail only. Drift 2½ Knots.

Dec. 18 At 2 P.M. it moderated to a Calm. Sent the top gallant yards aloft,
Shap'd our Course for the land, E.S.E. Wds Clears With a gentle breeze.—

" 19 At 7 o'clock, John Downs Cried Land, from the Mast head, bearing S.
by W. 8 leagues distance. at 9 Saw it off deck. the Wind being dead ahead no
prospect of getting in 'till tomorrow.

" 20 At 8 O'clock Saw land off Deck, 3 leagues distance. A Sail in Sight,
suppos'd to be an enemy, and bearing down upon Us. All hands preparing the
boats, the Captain being determin'd to run the Ship on Shore, rather than being
taken every man securing his duds.—At 9 P.M. lying off and on in the bay of
Pingasanon.—

" 21 At 9 A.M. Came to an Anchor about 2 Miles from the Village of San
Isadore in the province of Pingasanon,[74] on the Island of Luconia, one of the
Phillipine Islands, and about 400 Miles from Manila. At 11 Oclock the Captain
Went on Shore with four Men, and Peter Tellier, as interpreter, on landing they
were immediatly, secured by the Indians, and examin'd by the Officer of Government, Don Josse Lopez and After two days detention were liberated, the
inhabitants were fully Convinc'd We Were English, and that our intention Was
plunder. in consequence, they remov'd all their valuable effects consisting of—
Crosses, Roman Relics &c. into the mountains and alarm'd the Country for
many leagues. We heard a few days after, that there was as many as 1000 men
ready to receive us.—

On the 22. A Pilot Came on board With a Number of the Indians, to remove the Ship to a harbour more Secure from the Enemy, and About two miles distance.

our present Situation was indeed very much expos'd to Wind, Which often blew with great violence, during the Night, but in this harbour, it was represented, we shou'd be perfectly Safe, both from the violence of the Weather, and the sirch of the Enemy, and indeed on our Anchoring, We Could not help admiring the place, for its great pleasantness, and the Security it offer'd. It was, a Kind of Small bason, not More than three quarters of a mile in circumferance, Surrounded With very high Mountains, the intrance very narrow there being no more than 3 fathom Water at flood tide.

We Moor'd the Ship oposite the Village of Porto Sual about ½ mile from the Shore in Seven fathoms Water.

This Country is amazingly Wild, especially toward the Mountains, Which are heap'd upon the backs of each other, making a most Stupendous Appearance of Savage Nature, with hardly any Signs of cultivation, or even of population. All is Sublimity, Silence, and Solitude.

The Natives Who are bound to Spain, by the ties of the Catholic Religion, live togather in Glens and Vallies, Where they Are Sheltered from the Cold and Storms of Winter.

In St. Isador they have a Monastery, and Church, and in this place a Small Chapple. all the inhabitants wear crosses, and Rosaries, and their houses are universally ornamented with the figure of every Saint in the Callender.

December 24. An Order came from the Alcaldi, or Governor to unship our rudder and send it on Shore, and the Night After, by a false arlarm by the Governor of Sual, all our Guns Were Sent on Shore, and plac'd in line, fronting the entrance of the harbour. five men Were Sent on Shore every Night, as Sentinels. We suspected this was done to "hum" us, they still believing We were enemies.

on the 27 Dec. a fire broke out in the Village of St. Isadore, the Whole of it wou'd inevitably be consum'd had it not have been for the Ship's Company, Who exerted themselves greatly on this occasion. about twenty one houses were consum'd.

The next morning, We were visited by the Governor. The Padre, or Holy Father, and a large retinue of grotesque figures dreast in the ancient Spanish manner, with long Toledo's, daggar's &c. The Holy Father gave us his benediction and presented the Ships Company with two bullocks. the Governor gave us two barrells cocoa nut Wine, and invited the Captain to dine with him.

on their departure three Guns Were fir'd on Shore, by order of the Captain.

The people were very generous, and attentive, having a great respect for the Whites. they Seem'd to endeavour to emulate each other in pleasing us, treating us with Wine, fruit &c. Whenever we happen'd to be among them.

We remain'd at this place Waiting with great impatience for an order to Sail for Manila. We Rec'd no order untill the 31 January, [1809] When, after taking on board a Pilot we weigh'd anchor and Sail'd in the Evening.

February 2 At 10 A.M. Sprung our fore mast in a heavey squall, the Captain Carying a press of Sail to avoid the cruisers that may be on the Coast. on the 3d Saw a Sail about 2 leagues to leeward, made all Sail possible, at 4 P.M. Saw the Castle of Maravilles,[75] bearing S.E. by E. four leagues distance.

This Fortress is situated on an Island,[76] at the entrance of the Bay of Manila. it has a very formidable appearance, being plac'd upon a high Rock, inaccessible on all sides. it has six Towers, a Citedel, with triple Ramparts, with two Gates, each having a Portcullis, Which Are defended by about two hundred pieces Artilery each.—the Liutenant Governor Commands this place in time of Seige.

on the 4 at 8 A.M. Was boarded by an Officer from the Fort of San Lopez— at 10 pass'd Marravilles Castle, Was brought too by the fort, and an Officer came on board, Who treated us, politely.

At 12 P.M. Came to an Anchor in Seven fathoms Water, the City of Manila bearing W. 2 Miles distance.—the Cap objecting to discharge us at this place, (excepting giving us a due bill on the owner at Boston) I was advis'd to apply to Don Josse Blanco, Who being made acquainted with the affair, immediatly commenc'd a Suit against the Captain.

I in the meantime remain'd at Blanco's Who treated me with the greatest hospatality.

on the 28 February Blanco Advanc'd One hundred and ten Dollar's to the Atorney, Who Say's, that it Will be a long time before it will be concluded, but will eventually terminate in our favour.

On the 11 March, in Consequence of my Applying to the Custom house, the Captain gave Us a permit to take our Chests out of the Ship.

On going on board, I found my Chest broken open, and every Article of the least value taken out. Among them Was two Waistcoats, 1 pair of trowsers 1 Whole Seal Skin, three Volumes Books, and a number of Pearl, Shells, &c. from the Sandwich Islands.—most of the peoples Chests, were broken Open.

On the 13 March the Ship was nominaly Sold to a Spaniard and hoisted Spanish Colours—She Was taking freight for China. on the 15. The *St. Fernando.* (late *Amethyst*) Sail'd for Macoa, with about 30 Passenger's, and man'd by Indian Sailors.

J. C. O'Farrell Went as Supercargo, and Captain Smith as passenger, leaving the first and Second Officer's on Shore at Manila, and giving Security for the payment of our dues, Which We Shall have if Justice predominates.

March 25. Went into the Country With Blanco, on a visit about fifty miles in the interior. in this jaunt I was most inexpressably gratified, not So much from the pleasure of the Journey as from the free genuine, and unreserv'd attention, that I experianc'd, which God avert I shou'd ever forget.

We tarried here four day's, dining upon Ragouts, Pintadores,[77] frigasees, Olopodridas,[78] clearing the Passage with the best oil of the nut.

March 29. A Ship and Brig arriv'd from Calcutta, but were immediatly Seiz'd, in Consequence of the Governments not receiving any official account's of Peace.—

our law Suit Still continu'd to Swell into a Volumn—and will it is suppos'd be as famous as the trial of Count Lishamogo, and Squire Chumpio[79]—they Will (the Papers) however, be enroll'd in the Palace at Madrid!—April 15 Blanco made another advancment to the Atorney.

April 20 A grand fistival Was celebrated in consequence of Peace between Spain and England, and Fernando the Seventh's Coronation.

At 12 OClock, Te Deum Was chaunted in the Cathedral, before the Governor, Don Mariano Gonsalez Aurelez, and all the Cavelero's of the Cyty. After Which, the Benediction was given in an August manner by the Arch Bishop, then His Excelanza, with the arch bishop, the Abbots, and Supperior's of the different Monasteries, With their Crosses, relics &c. Were escorted to the Governors, Where they then partook of an Elegant Banquet.

I was told there was fifty thousand dollars, distributed to the Poor on this occasion.

In the Evening the Cyty, and Subarbs Were brilliantly illuminated, and A Grand display of fire Works Were exhibited—in the different Church Yards—

Manila is a regular built Cyty, of about two miles Square, double Wall'd intersected With ditches, and Morasses, and flank'd with sixteen Tower's. it has four gates, each defended by a bastion of ten Guns. A Major General commands the inner Gate, and dines With the Governor.

The Castle of St. Iago is the Principal fortress and is quite Strong. here all the State Prisoners are Confin'd. This is Commanded by a Major Who is also invested With another Office as Alcaldi, Comptroler of the Troop's, Inspector of the Prisons &c, and lives in great magnificence. there is also another person of "Gigantic Power" Call'd the "Commadante Del Marineros" Who Supreintends the Gun Vessele's, Boats &c. The Houses are built of Stone of a Moderate heigh, the Streets are decently Wide, very clean and tolerably Well lighted.

A Company of horse patrols the Cyty during the Night, but notwithstanding this precaution, Asassinations are very frequent.—

The Public buildings are all of the Ancient Order. that of the Inquisition, is a huge, gloomy, Gothic pile of dark Stone.—over the Outer Portal, is a figure of the Blessed Virgin, Which according to their tradition Weeps blood, on every Good Friday.—in this Recepticle, the torture, and all the forms of this infernal Order are Sanction'd—Some of the Churches are extreemly elegant, and ornamented with an imensity of Silver Plate, and a great number of European Paintings, Some of them very beautiful.

The Church of St. Augustine is a most noble building, of old times. it joins on the Monastery of the Same Name. When I first Saw them I thought it was the Inquisition. it maintains about three hundred Monk's, Who to appearance are no Strangers to good living, here is about six hundred Paintings done in Europe. Some are indeed very Elegant. The Death of St. Augustine, and St. Genevieve, are the Most Admirable Paintings I ever saw. The floor of the Church is Compos'd of Stone, Which cover's the Tombs of some of the Ancient families of the City. upon theese "tablets of Memory" are incrib'd the Name's and family of those deposited beneath.—

I was treated very civilly by the Superior, Who Apparantly, paid his devours to Bachus more than to the Cross. indeed all the brothers had he appearance of being more fond of a bottle of red Catalonia, than—"The Cruet of Pale Vinegar"

There is a College here, Wholly dedicated to Religion, no person is admitted, but what intend to take the Order's of the Church. exclusivly, the Latin language, The Knowledge of the Bible, and the forms of the Catholic Religion, are only taught, and here the Monk's and Tutor's use all their endeavours to persuade the Students, that happiness exists not Without the Wall's of a Convent. To deserve admittance into this Seminary, is the highest ambition. The instructors carefully repress those virtues Whose Grandeaur, and disinterestedness are ill suited to the Cloister.—instead of universal benevolence, (The beauty of Religion) they adop't a selfish partiality for their own particular establishment, they are taught to consider compassion for the errors of others, as a crime of the blackest die. the natural frankness of their temper are exchang'd for servile humility, and in order to break their natural Spirit, the Monk's terrify their young minds, by placing before them, all the horror's with which Superstition can furnish them. They paint to them the torments of the Damn'd, in colour's the most dark, terrible, and fantastic, and threaten them. With the slightest fault, With Eternal perdition.

Thus instead of endeavouring to make Religion clear and lucid, they entirely obscure it, With Monastic darkness.

What strikes a Stranger immediatly on going into Manila are the Church Yards, which are <u>ornamented</u> with monuments of human Skull's. the wall's especially, are Cover'd with the Sconces of Priests, Indians, and Cavelero's "grining Horridly" enough to impress the most insensible With horror and disgust. Nor do the people hesitate to exhibit fire Works within the pale of theese Relics. they might as Welt "Play at loggarts With them"—

The women of Manila are in general, ill looking, Pale, and destitute of that appearance of health, without which there cannot be perfect beauty. The Rich are very disipated, very much in the habit of Gambling, and more fond of being in the train of Venus, than Diana. they are equally in the habit, like the Indians of Chewing Beettle Nut, Which stains the teeth with the most disagreeable blackness. They dress without the least taste, and very indecent. So extremly thin is their drapery, that I have seen the movement of every muscle in their composition. They are also so void of delicacy, that it is quite common to see a Young Lady pay her Devours to Cloacina in the Street.

The Spaniards here, and the Indian's live in A State of perfect idlenouss and inactivity. The manufacturs, and all other buisiness is done by the Chinese, Which are Said to amount to upwards of eighty thousand. theese people exhibit a Striking Contrast to the indolence of the Spaniards. it is very Common to see them Sitting by the doors of their Shops, playing, at Cards, dice &c. So that it is as Strange to see a Chinese idle, as a Spaniard, or Indian imploy'd.—

There are no Kind of public amusments, excepting Riding, and Walking on the Prado which is fill'd with dancing Girls, and people of every discription every Night, till a late hour. here the Company are entertain'd with music, and every kind of fruit in perfection, Which can be had at a very Moderate price.

Provisions, and every Kind of living in Manila, is remarkably cheap, the, markets being Continually Stock'd with the finest vegetables and Meat in the World.

April 21. The Ship *Belle Savage*, late of Boston, arriv'd from South America. She Was taken on the Coast by the Spaniards—she belongs now to the Phillipine Company.

May 12 The Festival of St. Clemants, Which was celebrated with high Mass, and a procession of Monk's at Midnight.

May 15. Visited the Convent of St. Clario, in company with two Spaniards. the Grate is contriv'd with a large peice of ornamented Wood, which turns on a swivel, and intirly prevents the person from being Seen. The nun's generally put out their hand at the Side, when taking leave of their friends.

Here I heard the famous hymn to the Virgin, Which I always thought must be sublime, When Sung by the nun's, but in this I was greatly disappointed, the Sounds being Shrill' tremulous and discordant, appearing to be more for form Sake than Devotion or harmony.

on the 20 May a Brig belonging to the Phillipine Company arriv'd from Cavitto, bound to Acapulco, South America. Blanco exerted himself to procure me a passage home by this conveyance, providing me with all the necessaries of the Voyage and offering to draw on his friend in Lima in my favour, to the amount of 200 dollar's. the Padre and Captain Were quite willing I shou'd go, but on application to the "Commadante Del Marineros" for a passport, he objected, alledging I was no Catholic, of course no Christian? under theese circumstances, Blanco desir'd me to wait patiently, for another opportunity. William Brown, and Asa Hooper, being Irishmen, Were indulg'd with, a Passage, at 20 dollars pr. Month.

June 1 The two English Frigates, *Doris*, and *Lucre*, arriv'd from Bengal.

on the 2 June Blanco Was arrested, and confin'd in the Castle of St. Iago, on Suspicion of Conspiring Against goverment, the next day his whives Son, and governess, where also arrested, and the house Seal'd up.—went to Don Manuel Eglisiors.—on the 11 June the *Amethyst* arriv'd from Canton, twenty two days Passage. The Captain Advanc'd his Atorney one Hundred dollars. The law suit still progresses in—expence—size—and fame—14 June five of our Company, Ship'd on board the *Antelope* Man of. War Brig.

On the 26, All hands Ship'd on board the *Amethyst*, at 8 dollars per month July 2. Blanca was removed to the Court yard. I obtain'd for the first time permision to See him on Sunday. He appear'd as usual very cheerful, with an openess of manner, which Convinc'd Me, he Was without guilt. Imploy'd in dismasting Ship, intending to ship a new Main Mast, and oth[er]wise repair her. on the 10 July three Ships arriv'd from Bengal brought new's of War with France and Spain.

July 16 at ½ past felt the shock of an Earthquake, lasted about eight seconds. the Streets full of processions of Priests. Wind at E.S.E. Barsella Brownal sent to the Hospital.—at 'this time I was imploy'd at the Captains house Writing, While the rest were preparing the Ship for Sea. Nothing particularly occured all the Month of August.

September 2. Barsella Brownal died at the hospital. He belong'd to Wrentham, Massachusetts, and has been Sick a long time. Previous to his death, he took the Sacrement, and profess'd Catholicism, and Was in consequence burried in the Church Yard, belonging to the hospital. his expenses were defray'd by the Priests.

on the 9 September The Captain propos'd altering the Voyage to the Pelew & Feegee Islands, for Beach à la Mar,[80] and Sandal Wood. There being no other American Vessell here, We Were oblig'd to Consent, Which will make the Voyage eighteen Months longer.—the wages Were increas'd to eleven Dollars pr. Mo.—Blanco Still in Prison. it is expected he will be transported to the Province of Buleno. September 25. John Brooks, and Daniel Guy very Sick.

October 3. Jon. Roundy and G.M. Bartlett, Ship'd on board the *Antelope*, Man of War Brig, in a moment of Passion.

on the 7 October, every person, except myself and B. Simonds, left the Ship, and went down to Cavitio, about four leagues distance. A French Schooner arriv'd being taken on the Coast by the Gun boats.

11 October The Captain Went to Cavitio after the Men that absconded, and put them in prison there. Brooks very sick.

on the 13 the men Came up from Cavitio, under a guard, and were put in prison in Manila. A Ship Arriv'd from Bengal.

on the 21. The Men were releas'd from Prison, and Came on board the Ship. Sent Brooks into the Country—to Die—

on the. 28 October, early in the morning, A Canoe came along side the Ship, with an Indian Woman, and the Corpse of poor Brooks, who died the night previous. He being a Protestant, the Priests refus'd—allowing him a Grave— and we were obligtd to bury him in the Chinese burying ground, about three Miles Without the Cyty. He was a native of Lexington, Massachusetts.

On the 29, The English Frigate *Fox* arriv'd, and on the next morning two of her boats arm'd came on board to press.[81]

November 14. The Captain propos'd settling the law Suit on the following terms. To pay Blanco 411 Dollars to defray his expences—To pay 90 Dollars to Roderigue Lopez—and the expences of the papers, and Seals of Goverment, at the Palace, amounting to 60 dollars our names to be continued on the Shipping Papers of September 1806 as formally, in full force and effect.—Without Which he cannot depart from the Port.—

November 15. The *Baracuta* Brig arriv'd from Macoa. She brought news of Peace between England and America, and that there were twenty two American Vessells lying at Whampoa. on the 16 the Ship *Romanceita*, late *Belle Savage*, Capt. Fernando Tuldia Sail'd for Acapulco, So. America—by this conveyance I wrote home.—

Nov. 25 The Spanish Gallion *Santisirna Trinadada*, Sail'd for Acapulco.[82] The next day the English Fleet sail'd under convoy of the Baracuta Brig for Pulo Penang.[83] Saluted which was return'd from the Batteries.

on the 28 the *Amethyst* haul'd from the pier, and anchored off the Cyty.

imploy'd taking things on board and preparing for Sea. the next day the Phillipine Company's schooner (late belonging to the French) Sail'd for Acapulco, with dispatches. Commanded by Eben H. Corey of Providence, R.I.

December 4. Took an affectionate leave of Blanco at the Prison, who insisted on my taking 500 Segars & two dozen arrack.[84] At 3 P.M. Weigh'd the best lower anchor.

From Manila to the Pelew Islands[85]

December 6. At ½ past 11 A.M. Weigh'd Anchor, and Came to Sail with the wind E.S.E. at 7 P.M. pass'd the Castle of Maravilles. Was boarded by an officer.

on the 8 enter'd the Streights of San Barnadino.[86] With Westerly Winds and squally Weather, shall have to Come to an anchor for more ballast, the Ship being "flying light."

on the 16 at 8 P.M. Came to an Anchor in eleven fathoms Water, on the South Side the Island of Luconia. the Moorish Town of Lusitte bearing N. by E. and the Spanish village of Buleno[87] bearing W.—in the Evening a number of Indians came on board with Tobacco, fish, honey &c.

on the 17th in the morning, the Captain went on Shore, to the Padre's, who said that this place had not been settled more than ten year's. at present there is about five hundred inhabitants. it has a Church, and one Convent, Which togather with the Town make a very pretty Appearance from the Sea.

The interior country is Compos'd of Mountains of the most Majestic Grandeaur, cover'd with Wood's with Such a variety of Peaks and promentories, as to appear the Work of enchantment. We cou'd distinguish the Volcano of Monte Del Inferno, about six leagues distance, but could not at this distance observe the smoke, which continually ascends from its summit. in the Night, we cou'd just perceive a faint illumination in that quarter.

The Padre sent a couple of Goats, and some fowls, for Which the Captain return'd some Powder, and shott. Five men very Sick. on the 19 We were imploy'd in Setting up preventer Shrouds, on the Fore mast, it being found to be Sprung.

on the 20 December we weigh'd Anchor and Sail'd with a fair Wind. At 4 o'clock A.M. Monte Del Inferno bore W. by N. 16 leagues Distance.

We Continued in theese Streights untill the 29 When the Wind and tide being in our favour, We were driven thro it with prodigious Swiftness.

Theese Streights are universally known to be very dangerous, being in many places very narrow, and having a great number of Reefs and breakers, which stretch many miles from the Land. There is also a prodigious tide or Current

Which generally runs at the Rate of six or seven Knots, making it most impossible for a Ship to make any progress thro the Water. During this tedeous navagation, we had very tempestious weather, the Wind blowing in Violent squalls, accompanied with incessant rain, lightning, and labourious Sea's.

From the 16, When we anchor'd in Bulino, untill the 20th we had Gales. on this day we attempted to weather the Small Island Call'd "Madre D'Deos" but was necesiated to put back in consequence of the Violence of the weather and velocity to the Currents.

We Still however, continued persevering in our indeavours of obtaining an offing, Which We cou'd have effected with little trouble, with ten Hours free wind, but all our attempts were fruitless, and we were oblig'd to return, and anchor in the most Conveniant Parts of the Coast, expos'd at all times to the Land breezes, which often blew With the greatest violence during the night.

Here We lost one Anchor, and were in great danger of loosing our larger and only one, Which we drag'd in seventeen fathoms Water.

We were carried out with the greatest rapidity, the Wind & Current setting us at the rate of eleven Knots. At Sundown. the S.E. point of Luconia, bore W.N.W. Distance ten leagues.—

January 11, 1810 Came on a heavey Gale of wind and Rain from the N.E. which oblig'd us to lie too for forty two hour's, making a drift of 1 ½ miles pr. log. from S.W. to S.S.W. latitude 14.56. Sent all top gallants yards and masts below.

During this Tempest the Ship leak'd eight inches pr. the hour

on the 14 Calm winds, and variable. Daniel Grey and Hants Nelson at "Death's door," two others very Sick. on the 20 at about 10 A.M. Saw Land bearing from E. to S, seven leagues distance. The Pelew Isle's at 3 P.M. Sail'd between two Islands, endeavouring to make the Island of Corora,[88] Where the King liv'd. A Number Canoes came off to us. we took on board a Chief and eight others, to direct us the Way to the harbour.

22 January Strong gales and rain, a great number of Canoes arround us. they sail with the greatest velocity, going at the rate of eight miles pr. hour, directly in the Wind's eye. on the 23, we still continued to make but little progress to Windward. At 4 P.M. wore Ship[89] and Stood N. Daniel Grey in his last moments, two others were dangerously Sick, and several unfit for duty.

The poor Indian very much discourag'd and anxious to get on Shore. At night Stood to Sea ... on the 25 We Were Still endeavouring to come in with the land. by making too long taks off last night, we found ourselves thirty miles to Leeward.

At 9 A.M. Daniel Grey died.

All hands were in the greatest despondency, and nearly Jaded, and tired out. At 4 P.M. Came in With the Reefs. A great number Canoes arround us. a White man came off, and inform'd us that Corora laid sixteen leagues to Windward. Concluded to put in at the first Anchoring place if possible.

on the 26 Standing off and on the land, the Wind and Seas striving against us, two Canoes boarded us with fish, yam's &c. At 10 A.M. Consign'd Daniel Grey to the deep. for this purpose he was sew'd in a piece of Canvas and plac'd on a board, over the Waist rails. the Main Sail was then hove to the vast, to protract the Ships progress thro the Water, and he Was launch'd off.

At 5 P.M. a Chief came on board, Who inform'd, that the King Wou'd come on board tomorrow, provided a Man was sent on Shore as hostage. Accordingly George Leachit wast sent on Shore, laid off for the Night. All Grey's clothing and effects were Sold at auction, this afternoon. At 8 o'clock P.M. While Standing in, We discov'd Breakers directly under the Lee bow. Wore Ship immediatly and Stood N.N.E. at 12 P.M. Tack'd and Stood in untill ½ past 1, then Wore and stood off. The next day, We ran the reef along at S.S.W. untill 3 P.M. When we discov'd the Passage, and the King with a great number of Canoe's, with our man, coming thro it. At ½ past three, the King came along side in a War Canoe, beautifully decorated with Shells and paddled by thirty one men. Mr. John Lawson, was with him. he was left here to collect Beach a'lamar, by the Spanish Schooner, which left Manila the last August. He inform'd that the Passage was sufficiently deep to admit us thro it. We according tack'd, and stood off about half a mile, then wore, and put the Ship in the best trim possible.

We pass'd the two Points being not pistol Shots from each other. on getting thro this great danger, we were alarm'd by another equally as bad. The passage Stretching away Suddenly to the larboard Side, made it impossible to hold our Wind longer, and we had just time to stay the Ship,[90] and stand out again. the Surf running as high as the leading blocks in the rigging.

It is remarkable that there Shou'd be such an unsurmountable barrier encircling theese Islands. This prodigious reef lies about five miles from the Shore, and the above mention'd passage is the only one thro the Whole Coast, and thro Which a Ship must be oblig'd to pass, to obtain a harbour inside. We this Night Stood So far from the Land, as to be unable to discover it untill seven oclock in the Morning of the next day.

At 11 O'clock arriv'd off the entrance of the passage. the Wind being abeam, and the tide in our favour, we pass'd thro it, and after many "hair breadth escapes" from the breakers, being most intirly surrounded by them, got thro, Abathule, the King, being Pilot, and came to Anchor at ½ past one oposite a Small Village, about six miles from Corora, in eight fathoms water, the Village

Call'd Aragupsa bearing E. by N. ½ mile distance, and the two points S. and N.E. here we moored Ship and in the twilight, the King took his departure, with his Chiefs, Lawson &c. with one Musket, two axes, one Tokee &c. presented him by the Captain.

In the Evening a number Girls came on board, with no other dress, than what Nature gave them. they are much more dark than the Phillipine Indians, but more regularly featur'd. they Tatoo, or mark themselves, similar to the natives of the South Seas. they also paint the forehead red and use (like the Sandwich Islanders) Cocoa nut oil to perfume their persons. they are fond of ornaments to excess. on their wrists, arm's, and anckles, they wear bracletts of Turtle Shell. for a Rom.[91] or girdle, they have a String of Stones similar to carnelian, this they appear to value in the highest degree, as it is generally given them by a Favourite Youth. arround their neck's, they have a necklace of Pearl Shell, and What has a more pretty effect than the Whole, they ornament their hair, Which has a most glossy blackness, with flowers, as also their ear's which are perforated with a large hole on purpose.

Their teeth are very regular, but as black as ebony, caus'd by their being burnt, in their infancy, by the Parents—this they esteem as the greatest beauty, they possess. The Girls marry at about fourteen, but in general are too fond of Variety, to be faithful.

What is very remarkable, they have large buildings Some upwards of sixty feet in length, crowded with women, who are maintain'd by different individuals, of the other Sex, upon the same principals as the Cyprian Palaces[92] of Europe. over the Door is a huge figure of a Woman, carv'd in Wood, in the most obscene, and wanton attitude.

On going into one of theese places, one day, I found upwards of thirty young men lying indiscriminatly, in the arm's of their Dulcina's, envelop'd in a Matt. on my entrance, not One rose, but Seem'd to "cling tighter" to their companion—The Roof was ornamented with lemon boughs, evergreen &c. and in the avenues were baskets, of fresh fruit, tarro,[93] and honey in abundance.

No wonder, that this effeminate manner of indulging their pleasur's should enervate them to such a degree, as to make both sexes alike, as respect's Courage and prowess. their battles usually terminate, When ONE is slain.—however, this may be for the best, it is very seldom they are engag'd in War, for Here no person proud of his titles, or his Wealth, tramples under foot his humble countrymen, no cringing Valet flatters the vices of his Master. Man is equal to Man. Their enjoyments consist in the pure pleasure, that Nature offer's to her Children and their happiness is founded on the durable basis of mediocrity and equality.

The Country is most beautifully diversified with Mountains, hills and Vallies. What is rather remarkable, they cultivate nothing but the Cocoa nut tree, which grows here in great perfection. the tarro root, also is supreintended by the Women. all fruits peculiar to Warm Climates, grow here in great perfection.

on the 29 January, I went to Corora, with the Captain, with one musket and a few more axes for the King. Was receiv'd with great ceremoney. the King, Queen, and the Chiefs, being painted, infernally, and arm'd, with Spear's. His majesty, Sat upon a Stump of a tree (apparantly Cut for the purpose) which was cover'd with a Mat. the Chiefs, about forty in number sat arround, Cross'd legg'd on the ground.

We Were treated with fruit, Cocoa nut milk, and honey, which was presented by Girls of about six or seven years of age. The Girls entertain'd us with Singing, and dancing, Which Consists in putting themselves in the Most obscene attitudes. She that excells in this, is sure to meet with the most applause. I presented the queen with a String of beads, for which I was honoured in receiving "the fraternal imbrace" from her Copper Coloured Majesty.

February 4. The Armourer was imploy'd in fixing his forge, to alter the Chissels. the Indians disliking their taste.—there Appear'd but little Prospect of getting Beach a'laMar, at this place, and we imploy'd ourselves in overhauling the hold and preparing the Ship, to go further to Windward, to othre Islands, or else to Canton, the Ship being Considered incapable of going to the Feegee Islands.

On the 6 February, George Leachit, Samuel Baker, and Daniel Godsel, elop'd from the Ship while on their Watch the Night, in one of the canoe's alongside, with their Clothing &c. This reduc'd our company to eight men, who are able to work, the remainder being Sick, lame &c.

8 February. A great number of the natives on board, the Carpenter, Sam Leaman and Hants Nielson very Sick. at 6 P.M. two War Canoes went on Shore from Corora with a number Chiefs &c. "squally appearances."

On the 9 February at 5 o'clock AM, Hants Nielson died. Samuel Leam. and the Carpenter very bad. all hands very much discourag'd, it being very obvious, that we shall not be able to do any thing at theese Isle's and there being great danger of our being taken by the Indians, as there had been several meetings at Corora, between the King, and the Chiefs of the different Islands.

At 8 A.M. the Captain went to Corora, with some presents, the rest Wooding and watering the Ship. at 6 P.M. the boat return'd With a bullock. The next day, William Robinson ran away from the Ship. At 10 A.M. Abathule, the King Came on board, escorted by four War Canoes, of about forty men each. He remain'd on board about three hour's, and previous to his departure, desir'd the Captain to prepare a Feast, to morrow, on board, for him and twelve of his Chiefs. At one oclock above forty Canoe's came along side with Wood. as this was done without any intimation or desire from the Captain; it was ividently done to entrap us, and therefore all that cou'd hold an arm were order'd on Deck, and no more than one Canoe allowed to come along side at a time. this had the effect, we expected, for the Indians, seeing our preparation, some of them went on Shore without discharging, Which convinc'd us our fears were not without foundation.

On the next day, The King Came on board with his rupais, or Chiefs, with Above two hundred Canoes. Never While I live Shall I forget the appearance they made in Approaching the Ship. they were all in one exact line, and their paddles Keeping A Regular Stroke with each other, at every five or six minutes, they Wou'd all with great uniformity, flourish their paddles, and give a loud Shout, as in triumph. theese forms were ividently done to intimidate us, and I believe that most of us was sensible of a feeling, unknown before.

The Captain wou'd not permit, one of the Indians on board arm'd, and no more than what Came with the King. We had the tops man'd, matching[94] burning, and every man armed with a sword and brace of pistols. the Swivels on the taffes rail[95] were leveled forward, and loaded with thirty bullets each, and a man station'd at each with a lighted match with orders to fire directly among them on the least appearance of treatchery.

Abathule, the King appear'd Suppris'd at this preparation, and told the Captain. (by James our interpreter) that he [had] no thought of taking the Ship.

During the feast, which was on the quarter deck, every one was at his quarters, While the Canoe's laid a little distance from the Ship.

At about three o'clock, the King Order'd the Canoes, on Shore, to the Neighbouring Village, about ½ mile distance. this was artfully intended to Relieve us from the apprehension of danger which their presence might Create. At the Conclusion of the feast, at which a great quantity of Rum and Molasses were drank, We fired off the guns on both Sides, which made the Indians look rather blue, they being Charg'd to the Muzle with grape and Canister Shott. Soon after they left us, and Went on Shore at the Village intending to Sleep there for the Night. During the Night, All hands were on deck, with the Same order as before. the next day the King departed for Corora, without coming on board.—the Captain was now determin'd to be off as soon as possible. on the 14 February arm'd the boat, to go in Sirch of the men that absconded. At 10 P.M. return'd with only William Robinson, Who was immediatly put in irons, and confin'd below.

On the 14 February weigh'd Anchor, and remov'd about three miles, fronting the Seaward, more secure from the natives. the next day imploy'd in

sounding round the Island & finding a passage, the Islands being mostly surrounded by reefs, and breaker's. at 11 A.M. found a passage, but so very narrow,
as will make it impossible to go thro it, without a fair wind. the depth of water,
seven, nine and fourteen fathoms. This day was confin'd below unwell. the
Weather very rainy, and tempestous.

on the 16 the King came on board with two war Canoes. He propos'd to the
Captain, "that if he wou'd go to Artingel one of the neighbouring Islands, and
fight the King, Who is his enemy, and burn his Village, He wou'd procure a
Cargo of Beach a'lamar for the Ship."

The Captain then propos'd it to the people, who consented, on Condition
of receiving two hundred dollars extra in Canton, to be divided among 'em,
which was assented to by the Captain.

in the afternoon the King departed With his Chiefs. In the Evening Seven
Canoes came along side, with Goats, yams, Cocoa Nuts, &c. the King intending to go with us with twelve Selected Chiefs. At Sundown five War Canoes
arriv'd from Arabukah.

Feb'y 18. at 9 A.M. the King came on board, with George Leachit and two
others, that ran away on the 6 inst. and twelve Chiefs. they brought with them,
their Spear's, hatchets, and other Weapons with four Canoe's of yam's and other
articles.

At 11 Weigh'd Anchor and having a leading Wind, got thro the Passage With
safty. Some parts of it was so very narrow, as to perceive the Small Crabs, and
Cockles, crawling on the reef.

At 6 P.M. Corora bore West by North, eight leagues distance. Stood off the
land for the Night. on the 19 at 12 midnight, tack'd Ship'd and stood for the
Land, under easy Sail.—at 5 A.M. Saw Land bearing N.and N.E. by E. At 11
The Indians being very Sick, and it being very gloomy tempestous Weather.
The King told the Captain, that he had better put away again for Corora, it
being a bad season of the year for an expedition against Artingal, but promising A Cargo of beach ala Mar for the Ship, against the Season shou'd arrive,
that wou'd be more favourable to carry his plans into execution. The Captain
promising on His part to fulfil his promise of fighting Artingal, Which probably, we suppos'd would be about April or May.

At ½ past 1 Came thro the Passage, with the most eminent danger of getting on the reefs. At 2 Anchor'd in nineteen fathoms Water, Eru bearing E.S.E.
Malahi W. by N. and Corora N. by E.

February 22. We this day rec'd information, that the Above preparation was
purposly done to entrap us. The Ship on her Arrival at Artingal, was to prepare
the long boat for attacking the place. After the Guns were all discharg'd the

Chiefs were to demand their arms, which were on their coming on board deposited in the Arm Chest, and While the Captain was opening the Chest to deliver them, the King intended to dispatch him with his hatchet, which was to be a Signal for the Masacre of the Ships Company. there was to be there besides upward of two hundred Canoe's ready to receive us. It was thought that the Sickness caus'd by the Sea, discourag'd the King, and made him give up the Attempt. This information was comunicated by one of the Girls, who has been living on board the Ship, and who was at Corora, when the affair was first Contemplated. most of the Girls appear'd very anxious for the Men to go on Shore, and leave the Ship, a few day's previous to our Sailing.

March 4. imploy'd in preparing boarding Nettings,[96] fore and Aft, as high as the leading blocks in the rigging, and making barracade athwart the quarter deck. We this day made twenty two hundred musket balls, and prepar'd Seven hundred musket Cartriges, "two Centinels are plac'd on the quarter deck two on the forecastle, and one at the Gangway in the Waiste. the Same Watch is to be on Deck, during the Night as at Sea, and no Indian is allow'd (except the King) to come on board the Ship Arm'd. No honey, Shrub, or fruit (except Cocoa nuts, Marions, filberts Almonds.) are allow'd to be brought on board the Ship, except by the three FEMALES, AWANGA, UNGI AND ADRUA, blessings Sent from Heaven.

Portrait of King Abathule
of Palau. Collections of the
U.S. Library of Congress

Small quantities of Beach a'lamar are brought in by the Natives, and pur-chas'd by the Captain, with beads, and other small Articles. We hear nothing of the King relative to the Promis'd Cargo.

March the 9. The King of Arabukah came on board in the twilight He is a private enemy to Abathule, the King of Corora, but dare not declare it, for the Want of fire Arm's, the Corora King having Six to one. He promis'd us great incouragment, telling us he Wou'd procure us a Cargo of beach a'la Mar in four Months, if we would go to Arabukah. Previous to his departure, the Captain presented him with a Musket which he was very much pleas'd with, and in return—offer'd him his Wife.—He desired us to say nothing of his Visit, and at About twelve oclock, took his departure. his Canoe was pull'd by forty six paddles. He had about eight young Women with him, dreast in their best orna-ments, their hair decorated with the freshest, and most beautiful flowers. Three of the Girls, were really very hansome. The King Said, that the Women were all the Same at his Island, and could dance and Sing much better than the Corora Girls. It was very obvious that theese females, were Selected by the King that his invitation "might have the better grace."[97]

As we had but little prospect of doing any thing at Corora, the Captain was determin'd to be off in a few days, either for Arabukah or the Caroline Islands, about five degrees to Windward. the Ship Was in a bad Situation, both for Want of rigging, and Repairs in the hull.

On the 24. Abathule, the King came on board, with seven War Canoes. all hands were order'd under Arms. He appear'd very much disconcerted and did not tarry long. he brought with him about Seven picol[98] Beach ala Mar, A Bul-lock and Some other Articles.

At two o'clock the Beach a'la Mar huts on Shore, burnt up with about three hundred pieces in them, suppos'd to be done by the Native's. On the 25. in the Afternoon, the King of Arabukah, Came on board, and at four o' clock Lawson (the Manila Man) who has been taking B.L.M. at Pelelus, arriv'd. He said that he had been wholly imploy'd in Collecting it, since leaving us, but very little confidence can be plac'd in What he say's.

The Arabukah King appeared quite friendly, but we had reason to believe him Connected with Abathule. We heard for a Certainty that on the Ships arrival at Arabukah, they intended joining their forces togather, and attempt to take us.

The two White Men, who have been on theese Islands some years, and Who intend going home with us, were advis'd by their Wife's to come on Shore to Night, as the Indians intended Killing every one on board on taking us. the Captain Sent the three girls, Avranga, Ungi, and Adrua, to Corora, to try to

Drawing of a Palau Village. Collections of the U.S. Library of Congress

obtain Some information. What makes our Situation the more dangerous, is
the refractory disposition that Some of our Men begin to show. the Girls use
every mean in their power to induce the Men to leave the Ship, and go on Shore,
and live with them.

On the 31st March Jackie, the Kings brother of Corora, came on board with
two War Canoe's. he Said that his brother Wanted Us to stay, and fight Artingal, for which, we Shou'd have a Cargo of beach a'1a Mar. At about 1 hour after,
the King of Arabukah (Amaki) arriv'd, it appeared very obvious, they were Connected togather. previous to the Prince of Corora's departure, the Captain desir'd
him to inform his Majisty Abathule, that as he was unfaithful to his promise
in not getting Beach a'la Mar at this place, he shou'd put to Sea directly. The
King of Arabukah Went away the Same time, leaving us a pilot, to take us to
Arabukah.

On their departure, We fir'd a Gun, and set the Colour's, and at half past
two, hove up the Anchor, but finding We had drifted on a Shoal, let go again,
and brought up in five fathoms. in the Meantime, We examin'd the outer Reef,
and buoy'd the Channel. We found sufficient Water on the Reef to float the
Ship at flood, except in two places, where the Rocks, were just above the Water.

In the Evening, Saw a great fire, at the Beach ala Mar hut on Shore, and
Sent the boat to find out, what was going on, and found, to our great Supprise,

fourteen large War Canoes, lying in a line, full of Men. on going up to the hut, found their about twelve Chiefs, lying by the fire. on discovering our people they Were greatly Suppris'd, and Said, they Were going After Beach a'la Mar, and Were Waiting for the tide.

On hearing this the Boat return'd to the Ship. When We lighted our Matches, and hung a lanthorn in the main top. All hands on Deck during the night.

It appear'd evident their design was to us, shou'd We be so unfortunate, as to have got on the Reefs which they Knew, We Were fearful of.

April 1. At Daylight all the Canoe's put off from the Shore, standing for the passage, Which We was to thro. At five A.M. Weigh'd Anchor & Sail'd. on coming in with the Reef, Saw these infernal Deamon's, Waiting for us, their Canoes being fastned along side each other, in a line, but out the Reach of our Gun's.

At 12 P.M. got thro the Passage, and Stood to Sea, and here as if misfortune, Shou'd still follow us, we were detain'd nearly three hour's, in endeavouring to recover three Men, Who were upset in the boat, in going After A Canoe, Which got adrift. happily We took them on board in just Sufficient time, to Weather a Shoal, Which was about two miles distance on our lee bow. We however lost the Canoe, but got our boat in with some damage. At 4 P.M. Stow'd Anchors and Cables, and Settled the Nettings on the Rails. two Men continue'd very Sick, and four other's Confin'd to their births.

On the fourth of April We discover'd the Sun to be in eclipse,[99] from the begining to the time of its greatest obscuration, the Colour and Appearance of the Sky, Was gradually Changing from an azure blue, to a more dark and dusky Colour, untill it bore the Aspect, and gloom of Night. The darkness appear'd to come on regularly, and gradually, but the moment, the greatest obscurity was past, the light broke out, and increas'd with great lustre, and Splendour.

The Wind N.E. by E. a gentle breese, the land bearing from us, W. by N. and trending W.N.W. six leagues, distance, latitude 7.9.N. 135 E. longitude. At half past 11. had a little rain, at 7 P.M. Came in with the land, but being unable to Weather, it tack'd ship, and stood S. E. by E.

On the 11 of April Came too off Arabukah. this place like Corora, abounds with Reefs and Shoals, So that it was with great danger, We anchor'd in Safty. We anchor'd about two miles, from the Shore, it being impassible to go in further on account of the Reef's which lie in every direction.

At about three P.M. the Kings father (Tupia) came on board, and promis'd us every incouragment, but must not depend upon promises, at all events cannot take the Ship, if every one Acts with Conduct and fidelity. On Anchoring hoisted the boarding Nitting, and plac'd Centinels, as at Corora. On the thirteenth imploy'd in putting the Ship in the best posture of defence. Being surrounded with reefs, a retreat wou'd be impossible, if the Wind should fail us, shou'd an Attack be intended. At present the Natives appear'd quite friendly.

One Man very dangerously Sick, and two others unable to help themselves.

This day John Baldwin was detected in attempting to Elope with his "Wocosky"[100] He had a Canoe, drawn under the bows of the Ship, While the people Were at dinner on Deck, and Was just handing his Sumum bonum, thro the lumber Port, which by the bye, was rather too small for her hams, when they Were unfortunatly taken.—

on the 15 April Barsella Simonds died. he belong'd to Charlestown, N.H. in the East Saw a great fire upon the Mountains, Suppos'd to be Signals. Charles Bowen the Carpenter very low. this day got about two hundred pieces Beach a'la Mar. Some of our people imploy'd building a Hut on Shore, for to cure BLM [beach à al mar].

On the 29. Charles Bowen died. Was oblig'd to pay the Chiefs, five Chissels, to bury him on Shore. At Sundown, a number Canoes, came allong Side, with about 150 peices B.L.M. in each. Some prospect offer'd this day of our obtaining A Cargo, the Native's, having exerted themselves considerably.

On the 30. The King came on board, gave him One Musket, as Part Payment. he promis'd to load the Ship in Seven Months. Collected about 1500 pieces last night.

intend removing in further the first Wind, as We cou'd not possibly lie So far off Shore, being very much expos'd to wind, and our Cables, not being Sufficiently Strong, to stand much strain for any Space of time.

May 2 the Captain went to Arabukah with present's. Presented the queen, with Some Strings of beads, and Cocoa Nut Scraper's.

May 3 we heard that Abathule the King of Corora, Sent for Amaki the King of Arabukah to hold a Council. At 4 P.M. he return'd, When We learnt that the Object of this Conferance was to have the Advice of Amaki, Respecting an Attack on Artingal in a few days, as also another Village in the Neighbourhood, but We Strongly suspected that this Was but a mask intended to hide some treacherous Scheme preparing for us, as we have heard from good Authority, that Abathule had been here a few days since, on pretence of buisiness, in Seven War Canoe's, but that his real object was to prevail on Amaki to cut us off. Amaki appeared quite friendly, and Said he Would advise us When Abathule Wou'd arrive. however we was prepar'd to give them a warm reception, Should they have dared to molest us. At Present We defer'd going in further, untill affairs appear more promising.

two nights after We were alarm'd at about 12 o'clock, by Amaki and Dorr's coming on board, and informing that 170 Canoes had landed from Corora,

With Abathule, to fight Artingal tomorrow. Cast loose the Guns and had all hands on deck during the Night. Amaki Came on board to borrow a few muskets, from the Captain, but immediatly left the Ship, on Seeing this preparation. At 3 A.M. two others, of our men came on board.

At Daylight the King Sent to inform us there was no danger, and desir'd the Captain to Send Mr Dorr with the men to continue curing Beach ala Mar. at 9 they Went on Shore.

on the 10 heard that Abathule had gone to Corora Without fighting Artingal.

On the 12 May Weigh'd anchor at Daylight to move further in Shore. At 7 Oclock, Amaki, and Mr. Dorr came on board. A number Canoes assisted in towing the Ship in thro the Reefs. At about 4 oclock came to an Anchor in 16 fathoms Water. Arabukah bearing E by S 1½ miles distance. Aradmou SE. by E. 5 leagues, Uragalou ENE. 2 leagues distance. Shou'd the S.W. Monsoon Wind blow with any violence we apprehend great danger, being Surrounded With Reefs, within a Stones throw of the Ship, & our ground tackling[101] being very bad.

Theese Winds I believe begin to blow in the last of June and Continue untill December, accompanied with Taffoons [typhoons], or Sudden squalls of Wind, of about one quarter of an hour's duration, which lay's every thing before them.

On the 13 unbent the Sails.[102] the Natives took 4500 peices Beach ala Mar the last night. We this day heard that Abathule had offer'd large presents to Amaki to cut us off. the next day Sent the fore and mizen topsail yards on Deck, five hands on Shore curing BLM. At 3 P.M. Josse the Cook left the Ship, but Was Sent on board the Ship at Sunset. the next day he again attempted to abscond, and Struck the Centinel, at the Gangway, for which he was lash'd to a Gun, and receiv'd two Dozen with the Cat. On the 17 At night had a very Severe gale of Wind With great lightening. Sent all the yards and topmasts below. this Storm Created Such a Swell on the reefs as to prevent the natives from collecting any beach ala Mar for a number of days.

Friday May 19 heard that a battle had been fought between Abathule and Artengal, in which a number was Kill'd. the King of Arabukah's Son, a Chief of Corora, was Kill'd, in consequence of which no beach ala Mar Was taken for a number of days. The King, with his Chiefs &c. having gone to Corrora to be present at the funeral Ceremony, Which Will last Some time.

On the 24 The Captain went on Shore determining on knowing Wither he was to have any B.L.M. or not, as they have not taken any of consequence since the 12. The King told the Captain, that the Canoes shou'd go out as soon as the feasting was over at Corora.

At Sunset saw a number War Canoes, go on Shore from Corara, and a number also came this day, from other little towns friendly to this King.

The next morning Mr Dorr, and all hands, except a boy, Came off to the Ship, with a Canoe with some of the Chiefs, Who inform'd that a battle was to be fought to day (Wednesday) between them, and Ayalla, a Village joining On Artingal. Mr Dorr said that on Monday Night about twenty Canoes, full of men, arriv'd from Corora, and its neighbourhood, to assist in this battle. At Sundown A Canoe came Allong Side, and inform'd that Arabukah had been defeated with the loss of one man kill'd and Several Wounded. Imploy'd in Watering Ship &c. On the 26 Amaki Arriv'd from Corora. he Advis'd the Captain to Sail for Macoa, as it was impossible to procure B la M as Soon as Was expected, and leave one man here to supreintend getting it, the Ship to return in four months.

It is very evident they dislike our trade (having but a few Muskets) and take this mean to evade fulfilling their promises.

Sunday About 21 Canoes put off this Morning to get B la M on the Reefs belonging to Artingal. At 5 Oclock return'd, blowing their horns and alarming the people on Shore, who assembled in considerable number's, arm'd with Spears, hatchets &c. the Artingal Indians attack'd theese while on the Reefs, When a battle insued, in which the Arabukahs came off Conquerours, having Kill'd one man and wounded three. they brought 2200 peices B. la M.

May 27. heard that Artingal intended to attack us, which made us suspect another invasion from Abathule, it being impossible for Artingal to think of it.—

The Captain made Another proposition to Amaki, to get 1000 Sacks of B la M. he assented as usual, but little dependance Was plac'd in what he said. This day Sway'd up[103] our top masts, and began rigging the Ship, found our main topsail yard rotton, and condemn'd it.

Thursday The Carpenter found a place under the larboard Counter so rotton, Was oblig'd to cut a piece out of about a foot in length, and eight inches breadth. The next Day the Captain call'd all hands aft, to know their minds respecting going to the Feegee Islands. The hands objected, and demanded a Survey of the Ship. Accordingly a Survey was taken, by the following person's, by Appointedment, Mr Moses Carr, Chief Officer, Eben Dorr Second, John G. Olin, William Robinson, L. Coolidge, and James Barrett. After Which the following Memorial, or Protest, Was drawn up, and sign'd by the Ships Company, the Captain excepted.

WE the Officers, and Seamen, belonging to the Ship *Amethyst*, Seth Smith, Jun. Master, now lying at Anchor at the Pelew Islands, acknowledge to have Ship'd on board said ship, at Manila, to perform a Voyage to the Pelew, and Feegee Islands, but since our arrival, at theese Islands, (Pelews) having found the Ship defective in various Parts, her rigging most intirly gone, but one Anchor, and an insufficiency of boats, rendering her incapable of proceeding to the Feegee Islands, aforesaid, have thought it our duty, for the Safety, and benifit of ourselves, to demand a Survey of Said Ship, and have accordingly, with the consent of the Captain, Appointed propper persons, for that purpose, who have faithfully and impartially examin'd into the affair, and depose on oath as follows.

That the Planks under the Counters, are most intirly rotton.

Between the fore and main Channels, on the larboard side, nearly six feet rotton, this being Where the Sheathing is off, cannot tell how it is, where it is on. The Sheathing being intire on the Starboard Side, did not examine it particularly.

The Main beam is very defective, it working nearly 2 ½ feet.

All the Staunchions, are very much decay'd, and partly Rotton.

The Main Swifture is gone, no rigging for new one, and All the Rigging not Seaworthy.

We have no boats, but one Anchor, and but a small compliment of Men, having lost

Six, since our Arrival at theese Islands.

Under theese circumstances, We think we can, and DO refuse to comply with our engagments of going to the Feegee islands, and think it advisable to bear away for the first Port.

Sign'd
by the
Ships Company.
Pelew Isles June 1, 1810.

The Captain after expressing his desire of proceeding to the Feegee Island, and regreting the failure of the voyage, Concluded to prepare the Ship for Macoa. The Next day brought the Beach a'lamar off to the Ship, that had been cur'd on Shore by our people, amounting to thirty three Sacks, about fifteen picol. in the Afternoon the King with all his chiefs, came on board, to Settle for it. the Captain offer'd him one musket, about Seven Pounds of powder and 150 bullets. The old King Refus'd taking them, and Said he would make the B la M a present to the Captain, Who to avoid any dificulty gave him another Musket, Which did not Wholly content them.

Amaki wanted Mr Dorr to go to a feast at Arabukah, on purpose it Was suppos'd, to get an opportunity of stealing the things on Shore. At Sundown brought off the two cauldrons from the huts. The next day found that the Natives had taken one Cauldron, and one Iron pot, that was left on Shore last night.

Thursday George Leachit left the Ship. at 10 haul'd out the inside Reefs. At 3 P.M. came to an anchor fronting the sea board, in eleven fathoms water. Arabukah bearing W. by S. 2 leagues distance.

June 3. John Baldwin, elop'd with his Helen, a Young Girl, Who has been staying with him since our first arrival at theese Islands. This day we had every reason to believe the Natives intended to attempt taking us, as every Canoe was arm'd with an unusual number of Spears. We took notice also of their having a number of Muskets with them, and some catrige boxes, which the Captain presented the fling a few day's Since.

At 3 P.M. Came to Sail with the Wind S.E. at 5. got thro the Reef's, and Shap'd the Ships course for Macoa, that being the most convenient Port.

At Sunset, the Land bore E. by S. distance four leagues, the Ships course N.W.

Saturday June 9. At 11 A.M. Saw land bearing from W. to W.N.W. ten leagues distance, the Island Luzon or Luconia, the East Side. Haul'd N. Latitude 16.15.135 E. Longitude.[104]

June 13. got thro the Streights of Luzon[105] (which we enter'd on the 10) taking our last departure from the land. at Sun Set the point of St. Boxadore[106] bore E by S. distance five leagues, our course W.S.W. latitude 18.45. N. 119-25 E. Longitude.

Sunday June 16. at 2 A.M. Sounded in 87 fathoms, black and speckled Sand, with shells. The Coast of China. At 7 Saw Pedro Bianco,[107] bearing E. by N. six leagues distance.

This Rock the Captain Supposed to be The Grand Ladrone, and in consequence, Kept the ship away before the Wind. At about 11 Saw the Land, which prov'd to be the Mountains Surrounding Brandons Bay,[108] nearly ONE HUNDRED miles to Leeward of Macoa. This very unfortunate mistake Oblig'd us to haul upon the Wind, and stand to Sea, to the great Sorrow, and discouragment of all hands. the Weather very squally, With great rain.

Wednesday 18 June. This day We had three Taffourns, or hurricanes, in one of Which, We Split our main and mizin topsails, intirly to Shreds. Sprung our Fore Mast, and Carried away the fore topmast. At one time the Ship Careen'd So much, that her Main Yard Was in the Water. at that moment, which was about eight oclock in the Evening, We expected to carry away every mast by the board.—both pumps were Kep't going during the Night, and so exhausted were the people, that immediatly, On being reliev'd by each other, they Wou'd throw themselves on deck, and fall directly into a sound Sleep. We being Surrounded by the land, and the rock Pedro Bianco being Not far distant, our Situation was peculiarly dangerous. Theese Taffoons last about ten minutes, blowing with inconceivable violence. The next morning the Captain Call'd all hands Aft, and Propos'd trying to make a harbour to repair, which Was readily assented to.

There being a great number of Ladron's inhabiting this Coast, it was policy in him, in first submiting it to the people.

Thursday 19. June. Continued Stormy, Untill five P.M. When it moderated. continued to Stand into the land untill 7 O'Clock When We came to an Anchor. Feukien Point,[109] bearing E by S. 2 miles distance, here We repair'd our Sails, and rigging, for another rencontre with Boreas. A great number Chinese fishermen live here, their huts being all along Shore. At the Westward Saw a Fort and on one of the fountains A Watch Tower. Nothing can be immagin'd more desolate and gloomy, than the appearance of the Mountains, and the interior Country.

This being the Winter Solstice, and the Change of the Monsoon's, the Mountains were most always envelop'd in Clouds, which Were hurried over, their peaks, by the Violence of the Wind.

June 22 hove up our Anchor at Daylight, and departed with little hopes of reaching Macoa. Our Ship rotten, The Men jaded, and discourag'd, and in great danger of being taken by the Ladrons, or being blown to the Coast of Japan— Untill the 28 We had been Striving to Weather the Point of Feukien, somtimes gaining and at others lossing, and being Oblig'd to Come to Anchor.

At 8 in the evening of this day by unwearied persevirance, having Come to an Anchor during the day, no less than five times, got round the point, and Stood with. a fair wind for the lima passage.

Friday 29. the Wind Still Continued Easterly. At 11 A.M. Saw a number large boats, Carying Guns, Suppos'd to be Ladrones, and prepar'd to defend ourselves. they however did not molest us.

At Sun down the Grand Lima bore S.S.W. ¼ W. at ½ past 1 on the morning of the 30th. Saw the Grand Ladrone,[110] bearing NW about four leagues distance. This is a Rock of about a mile in circumferance, and is a Noted Sea Mark for mariners, in approaching the Coast of China. Ship's invariably take their departure from this Rock, when bound to sea.

At 7 A.M. made Macoa, the Castle bearing WNW four leagues distance. at about 9 Came to an anchor in four fathoms Water in the Typer river, the Cyty bearing N.E. the Castle E. three leagues distance.

Macoa is Still in possesion of the Portuguese, but intirly under the influence of the Chinese. it has a very formidable appearance from the Sea. Here the famous Portuguise Poet, Camoens, wrote the Lusiard [*Lusiads*]. We learn'd at this place, that no Americans had arriv'd this season, it being generaly suppos'd to be War with England and the United States.

July 2 A Portuguise Ship arriv'd from Bengal. they inform'd that an expedition was on foot, to invade Macoa with 10,000 troops. they Were to sail the Day after the Portugin.

On the 3 July A Survey was taken on the Ship, but nothing concluded on. July 5. Sent Samuel Leman, Who had been sick since the 11 December, to the Hospital. we heard that Edward Lawson, who left us at Manila in June 1809 had died in this Hospital.

July 7. The Ship *Trumbull* arriv'd from America. Saw a number of the NY. Evening Post,[111] which mention'd the probability of a War, with the United States and G. Brittain.

July 8. At about 4 P.M. A number of Portuguese Officers, came on board, and ordered the Captain, and first Officer out of the Ship, While they took a Survey of her Condition.

They opened the Starboard side, and found a place near the Mizen chains very rotten. After being on board nearly two hours, they departed Saying "El Barco vene Kil por el provedencia De Deos"? The Ship had come here by the providence of God.—

The Next Day, by order of the Governor, and in consequence of this Survey, We weigh'd anchor and came off Macoa, with a pilot, and anchor'd under a small Battery, the Convent Parie bearing N by E. The Castle Monte NNE. and the Cyty N-½E. distance about 2 miles. on the 12 the pilot came on board by order of the Governor (meerly to create an expence) to take the Ship further from the Cyty. At ½ past five came to an anchor about four miles from the Town, the Castle bearing W. two. miles distance. A Ship arriv'd from Pulo Penang the Next day. A Chinese pilot came on board to examine the Cargo, it being suspected (pretty Correctly) that the amount was not sufficient, to authorise him, taking the Ship to Whampoa. No pilot being Allow'd to take a Ship without having the value of Six thousand Dollar's on board. Previous to the pilot's coming on board we Were imploy'd in putting the beach a'la mar, in bread pipes, which contain'd two thirds of bread, which had the desir'd effect, We having the Appearance of a valuable Cargo on board.—

July 15 Samuel Leman died at the hospital, after taking the Sacrement, and professing himself a Catholic. He was burry'd very decently in the Church Yard. He belong'd to the State of Vermont, and Was a generous, good hearted fellow.

On the 17 July the Captain came on board with a pilot, got under Way, and came to Sail, the Wind blowing a Gale. At 9 P.M. Anchored in four fathoms Water, at the Nine Islands.

The next morning at Daylight got under way, and departed from Macoa bearing W by N, 3 leagues distances at 10 evening, Anchor'd at the Boca Tigres,[112] one half mile from the fort. The Pilot went on shore to obtain a Passport.

next morning got under weigh, and Pass'd two Forts, where we took a Mandarine, and arriv'd at Whampoa at 5 P.M.

We had Scarcly enter'd this famous river, When We were surrounded with boats, or rather Washing tubs, each containing a Tarter Girl, but What Suppris'd me most, was their thourough knowledge of the English language, which they Speak very correctly.

Theese Girls are mostly Supported by the Sailors, Who give them their clothes to Wash and mend and Which is done in a faithful manner. Guard boats continually pass up and down to prevent the Women from having any illicit connection with the Ships, but for all this precaution, "the genius of the Woman is predominant." on the 19, The Captain went on Shore with his papers, &c. the rest mooring Ship, and dismantling her.

August 3'd. the Ship Was Sold to Mr. Peter Dobell, for Six thousand Dollars, and on the 6 day following All hands were discharg'd and Paid off.

During my stay in Canton I boarded at Meegee's Coffee house, in Company with Mess. Carr, Dorr & Olin.

The Society in Canton is confin'd to a set of "Sour, unrelenting, money loving Villains" Who laugh at the Misfortunes of humanity. Not the least confidence can be plac'd in an European, American, or Chinese. If a Stranger speaks to an European or American, He will be treated with the utmost indifferance, excepting He has 10,000 Dollars, or 500 picol Beach ala Mar to dispose of.

If He goe's into a Chinese Shop, to purchase an Article, He must have as many eye's as Argus, to prevent, being fleec'd. Their Whole Study Seems to be to defraud, deceve, and Steal.

Their Poor, which are very numerous, present the most distressing Objects of human misery, and so insensible are the Chinese to their wants and Afflictions, that I one day saw a Man, throw out a parcel of potatoe parings, offals &c. to a most miserable Creature, with as much indifference, and Contempt, as if he was feeding a Swine.

The Women, that I chanc'd to see, excited in me no attention, but of Curiosity. I beheld them with the eye's of a Stoick. I would not have given my Pelew Indian Girl, for all the Women in the Chinese Empire.

No thing cou'd be more melancholy than my Situation. No prospect of getting home presented itself. I was confin'd to a dull room, without the least social, or friendly intercourse, in anxious suspence, for every future week. Our funds were So small as to afford but a "light Table," and "Small Cups." in the Month of September Mr. Carr left us, being unable to bear his Part.

September 22. Peter Tinkhan, late of the *Amethyst*, Was drown'd in Whampoa river. "We are such stuff as dream's are made of, and our little life, is rounded With a Sleep."[113] It is very remarkable that at most every place We have touch'd at, We have been oblig'd to pay duty, to Inexorable Death—

During the month of October, Several vessells arriv'd from America, and our Men, Who was generally Sup-ported by the Consul at twelve Cents pr. Day! imbrac'd the opportunity of getting home, but on Applying to the Master's, they were preemtorily Refus'd admission on board the Ships.—of their HUMANE COUNTRYMEN. in the exigency of the times, they being in a most Starving Condition, they as a last recource appli'd to the ENGLISH and Were Welcom'd on board, and treated with great hospitality.

On the 11 November, Olin left us, and Ship'd on board an ENGLISH Ship bound for Bengal, as Second Officer. By the liberality of Captain Smith, Dorr, and Myself were enabled to stand the brunt until the 25 November, When by the influence of the Consul, We obtain'd a Passage on the Ship *Chinese*, Brum, bound for New York, on Condition of Paying ten dollars each, and Working before the Mast during the Voyage. Mr Carr 'Went on board the Ship *Hope*, on the 20 on the same Conditions. Captain Smith Was oblig'd to give four hundred & fifty Dollars for a passage on the Chinese.

November 28. Sail'd from Whampoa at about 10 A.M. left the Ship *Atualpin*, belonging to Boston, and a number southern Vessels.

December 1 took our Departure from the Grand Ladrone, bearing E. NE. five leagues distance. on the 3. took a fresh Breese, and ran across the China Sea at the Rate of 10 Knots pr. hour.

December 10, enter'd the Streights of Banca,[114] with head Winds, and Rainy Weather. on the 17, pass'd the Sisters, 2 Small Islands bearing E. by N. two leagues distence. made Sail for Princes Island, but was oblig'd to Come to an Anchor, at Sun down, the Wind being ahead, and very tempestous Weather. December 18 head Winds, and squally, With incessant Rain, came to an Anchor occasionally, 2 men Sick. On the 19 inter'd the Streights of Sunda.[115] At Sun Set Saw the Cacataw Mountain bearing S. seven leagues distance, end

Tamarine Island W by N. 9 leagues distance. Saw two Sail, suppos'd to be Mala[116] boats. On the 22 got thro the Streights, and Stood for Sea. With Rainy Weather, untill the 23, When We struck the S.E. trades, Our Course being S.S.W. ½ W.

January 5, 1811, found our main Mast Sprung, abaft the trusses, imploy'd ficking it.

January 27. Saw the Coast of Africa bearing N by E. seven leagues distance. the next day Saw Cape St. Aguillas,[117] distance six leagues, sounded in forty fathoms Water. at ½ past 4 P.M. Saw a Sail, Standing out the land, on the 29 Saw A brig Standing to the Westward. A Short Allowance of provisions.

On the 12 February Saw a number of Tropical birds, and Cape hens. Caught a porpoise, February 13. Saw St. Helena.[118] bearing W½ N. Distance 10 leagues. A 5 P.M. Came to an Anchor in twenty fathoms. oposite We found here the Ship *Mary* of Newbury Port, Capt. Baldwin, and the Schooner *Ann* of ditto. Also one English, and Seven French Frigates, taken at the Isle of France. they Were bound to England direct. We heard that this Isle Was taken by the English, under the Command of General Abercrombie, with the loss of Sixty Men. All American Property Was confiscated. On the 15. having Water'd and taken in Some Salt provision &c. We Weigh'd Anchor and departed, our Course NNW½W. We took an American Passenger.—

St. Helena is a prodigious Rocky barren Island of about twenty eight miles in circumferance. The Town is very small, Situated between two dreary Mountains, and is well defended by Forts and Batteries. here is a neat Church, and I was told that a Theatre had lately been erected, by the E-I Company,[119] for the amusement of the inhabitants of this melancholy spot.

Tuesday February 22 at 7 A.M. Saw the Island of Accension bearing NE distance 19 leagues. At 12 meridian, Saw a Sail to Windward, apparantly standing for the Island. At 6 made the South of the Island in company with the Ship which prov'd to be the French Cartel,[120] We left at St. Helena. At about 8 P.M. Came to an Anchor oposite a White Sandy beach, but having drifted, tide were Oblig'd to heave up again after Which, we Stood off and the land With short tacks, in the mean While, the French Ship Came in and Anchor'd.

At about 9 Sent our boat on Shore for the purpose of getting Turtle.

At about 11 oclock Captain Smith, Who went on Shore with the boat, came on board and inform'd that the French Ships boat was on Shore, and had taken by force of arm's, the Turtle that our people had taken. they had Also taken a brace of Pistols, and a Musket, belonging to our Ship, had conducted in the most infanous, and cowardly Manner, threatning to Shoot our people &c.—

Captain Smith inform'd an Englishman, on Shore, Who appeared to have some authority that unless the Turtle, and arm's were given up, We Shou'd use force to obtain them.—Soon after this, the Frenchmen went into the Mountains to Kill Goats, without giving us the least Satisfaction.

Unwilling to bear this insulting Conduct with impunity, Captain Smith Was dispatch'd on board the Cartel With a Note to the Captain, Which Was also treated with great indifferance.

We now prepar'd to receive Satisfaction by force, and, accordingly, Got our Guns run out, the Captain being determin'd to fire into her, but not Without giving them every opportunity (considering She Was a Cartel) of making Reparation.

At 10 A.M. Wore, and haul'd along side within half pistol Shott of the Ship, and hail'd her, desiring the Captain or Chief officer to Send on board the property taken, Or else We wou'd sink the Ship. They Replied that they Were intirly ignorant of the affair, that the Captain, and all the boats, were on Shore &c.

Captain Brum answer'd, that he would give them two hours to consider of it. The Frenchmen desir'd Captain B. not to fire, as there Were a number of Women and Children on board, that the long boat should be got out, and they Wou'd come on board.

In about an hour After, their long boat came along side, with four French Officers (Who We afterward understood Were the General and his aids) dreast magnificently. After a great number of Conge ala Mode D. St. Cloud,[121] they inform'd by their interpreter, that they Were extremly Sorry for the dissagreeable buisiness, that had occu'rd, and that they were Willing to make any Reparation in their Power, that it was done intirly without their Knowledge &c. &c. they said that the Ship was own'd by an Englishman, who Was now on board, that She Was commanded by an Englishman, and that this infamous transaction, must have been done by their orders. That as there were a number of Women & Children on board the Cartel, it wou'd be the means of distressing them, without doing ourselves any essential benefit, shou'd we attempt to injure the Ship, that finally they wou'd Return on board and use their influence in endeavouring to recover our property. Captain Brum then invited them into the Cabin, and on their departure, Mr. Cole presented them, with some Sweetmeats, for the ladies. The General was arm'd and dreast in an elegant style. He wore A Star, and Red Ribbon in his left button hole and Was a very hansome man—He appear'd very Sorry at the Conduct of the English. They were set on board their own Ship by our jolly boat. The General presented the boats crew, with ten Dollars.

At about 1 o'clock, the French boat came again along side, with an ordinary looking animal half drunk, Who call'd himself the Captain, and Said he was suppris'd at our conduct in threatning to Sink his Ship, and that if we attempted to, we might find ourselves mistaken, and us'd very abusive language.

Finding We could get no satisfaction, and being unwilling to loose the Wind, we made Sail, our Course NW¾N—February 24. Saw a Brig standing to the Northward and Westward.

March 1 at 11 A.M. Saw a Sail Standing to the Westward. At 4 P.M. Cross'd the Equator, and Pass'd into North latitude.

On the 4 March Struck the N.E. trade Winds. the Steward confin'd in Irons, and put in the run, for Striking the Captain, Who is a man "that uses power, but forgets right."[122] March 12 At 6 A.M. Saw three Sail on our weather beam, apparantly a Frigate, With two prizes. March 14 Saw great quantities of Gulf Weed, and Some tropical birds. bent new Sails in preparation for bad Weather. on the 9 March an Eclipse of the Moon. Owing to the inatention of the Starboard Watch I had no opportunity of observing its begining. At 12 When I Was Call'd, the Moon was half obscur'd, and Continued untill two, even the Officers were so incurious, as to decline this opportunity of ascertaining the Ships longitude, which might have been determin'd with minute exactness.

On the 17 March enter'd the Gulf Stream, when we had a Gale at NE. which continued about fourteen hour's, the Sea making a Clear breast over the Ships deck. At 6 Sprung the for top gallant Yard. Saw a Ships topmast float Past us.

March 20. Sounded with 130 fathoms line. No bottom. March 30 found Ground with 52 fathoms. Grey Sand. April 1 Sounded in 14 fathoms. Sand With Shells. Weather very hazey and rainy. Saw a Ship Standing to the Eastward. April 2. Saw Land bearing NNW 3 leagues, the highlands of York.[123] at 9 A.M. took a pilot. April 3. Arriv'd at the City and Anchor'd.

1811 April 3
1806 Sep 17
4 Years 6 mo. & 17 days

A long yarn! & an old Salt!
Much to learn & no Fault.

David Christie	drowned	Scotland.
Silas Helem	Eloped	Stonington, Con.
Alexander Walker	ditto	Barry, Mass.
Caleb Whitman	died	"
William Ford	Eloped	England

James Pease	do.	do.
Thomas Jackson	do.	Concord, Mass.
Libia Pratt	Do.	Do.
Artuai	died	Sandwich Islands.
Peter Richardson	died	Westford, Mass.
Stephen Howe	died	Amherst, N.H.
Atooi	died	Sandwich Islands
Sages.	died	do do
Leoi	died	do do
Thomas Rutt	eloped	N. H.
Charles Abby	eloped	
John Downs	eloped	England
Asa Warden	eloped	England
John Garrison	eloped	Boston
John _____	eloped	Cape Cod, Mass.
William Brown	eloped	Ireland
Asa Hooper	eloped	Ireland
Barzilla Brownal	died	Wrentham, Mass.
Jon Roundy	eloped	England
Geo. M. Bartlett	eloped	Ny. Port Mass.
John Brooks	died	Lexington Mass.,
Daniel Grey	died	England
Geo. Leachit	eloped	England
Samuel Baker	Ditto	Do
Daniel Godsel	Ditto	Do
Hants Neilsen	Died	Denmark
William Robinson	Eloped	England
Barsilla Simonds	Died	Charleston N.H.
Charles Bowen	Died	New Haven Con.
Josse _____	Eloped	S. America
John Balainette	Eloped	Italy
Edward Lawson	Died	Boston
Samuel Leman	Did	Vermont
Peter Tinkham	Drowned	Mass.

Lewis Coolidge, most unfortunate of all, arriv'd safe at Boston.

| Editor's Note

At the end of Herman Melville's *Moby-Dick*, his narrator, Ishmael, says: "And I only am escaped alone to tell thee," which comes from Job 1:15–19.

At the end of his journal on the voyage of the *Amethyst* from 1806 to 1811, Lewis Coolidge lists all members of the crew who sailed from Boston, telling what happened to each one, and then says on landing again at Boston: "Lewis Coolidge, most unfortunate of all, arriv'd safe at Boston."

This was some forty years before the 1851 publication of *Moby-Dick*.

2

The Fur Seal Trade with China in the Early 1800s

Lewis Coolidge and the rest of the crew of the *Amethyst* left Boston in 1806 with the intention of capturing fur seals and selling the fur skins in Canton, China. During the voyage, they added another export commodity, bêches-de-mer or sea cucumbers, a trade item prized in Chinese cooking. In return, with the proceeds from the sale of those products, they intended to purchase Chinese tea, porcelain, silk, and other items available on the Chinese market that would bring a good price back in Boston.

The choice of China as a destination for the *Amethyst*'s trade goods was not a casual decision. In the early years following the American Revolution, Britain was still the primary trading partner for the United States, but few other ports were open to American merchants. The British had closed off most of Europe and virtually all of the Caribbean, partially out of spite for the Revolution but also because of the resumption of the Napoleonic Wars in 1803. Following the new hostilities between Great Britain and France, both the British and the French instituted restrictions on trade wherever enforceable to deny war provisions to the other belligerent party. In 1805, in what became known as the Essex Case, Great Britain ruled that American cargo was subject to seizure unless the trade was between two American ports, further inhibiting the free passage of American ships on the high seas. Spanish control of Latin America left few opportunities for trade there other than basic provisioning.

China, although halfway around the globe from Boston and other American ports, was one of the few possible trading partners for the new republic. China held great appeal for trade, both historically and in the early days of the American nation, because of the precious commodities available for sale there and nearby. The discovery of America was, of course, a serendipitous by-product of a search for trade routes to the Indies to obtain those commodities. Christopher Columbus named the Caribbean islands "Indies" by mistake.

Statue of Missouri senator
Thomas Hart Benton. From
the collection of J. Felt

After the recognition of the American continental land mass, the appeal of the Orient continued as explorers sought efficient land and water routes across the American continent with the hope of better routes to China. President Thomas Jefferson commissioned Lewis and Clark to embark on their epic journey to map the vast Missouri River Basin but also with the goal of finding a water route to the Pacific to improve on the lengthy time involved in the dangerous trip around Cape Horn to engage in trade in the Orient. The statue in St. Louis of Missouri senator Thomas Hart Benton, an avid proponent of expansionism in the early republic, has him facing west with the inscription at the base of the statue reading, "There is the East. There lies India."

Chinese tea was a prized commodity in the new republic, with still-fresh memories of the Boston Tea Party and heavy taxes on tea that would no longer have to be paid to the British. The tea thrown overboard at the Boston Tea Party was, after all, Chinese tea. Porcelain and silk were also of great interest. Cotton cloth, called "Nankeen" from its production point near Nanking, was another early import from China. Indian cotton was imported into China and transformed into readily usable "Nankeen" fabric. By the mid-1800s, the direction of the cotton cloth trade would reverse, as the great cotton looms of Lowell,

Massachusetts, and other New England towns would give American cotton cloth a dominant position in the world. From the late 1700s through the early 1800s, however, Chinese Nankeen cloth was a profitable import for American traders.

The Chinese regulated all aspects of foreign trade, including where the ship was to be offloaded and which Chinese could act as buyers of the imports and sellers of the exports. Canton was designated by the Chinese government as the only foreign trade port. The Manchus, in power since the 1600s, did not see any advantages for them deriving from foreign commerce. They viewed themselves as a superior people and were content with their world. The Chinese would contend that they had the best drink in the world—tea—and the best fabric in the world—silk. The emperor expressed disdain for the petty machines of the westerners. With this outlook, Chinese authorities attempted to limit the influence and impact of the foreign traders, who were relentless in their approaches to the Chinese market.

For fourteen months beginning December 22, 1807, the United States instituted its own embargo on foreign trade. The purpose of this embargo was considered to be to punish England by denying American raw materials because of England's depredations on the high seas in which they impressed American seamen. Fortunately for the *Amethyst*, all ships already on the high seas were exempted from the order.

In the first years following the Revolution, the Americans had few goods with appeal in the international marketplace, let alone in the Chinese market. The economy was largely rural with few manufactured goods. Farmers produced rice and tobacco, which had been major exports to England and other countries in Europe, and the lumber from the vast American forests was sold on a limited international basis. As noted above, years would pass before American cotton and cotton cloth would be a valued export.

The first significant American export commodity was ginseng, prized by the Chinese for its reported medicinal qualities. The American variety grew wild in the forests of the eastern United States. It was considered interchangeable with Chinese ginseng and available in quantity at significantly cheaper prices than Chinese ginseng.

In *The Old China Trade*, Francis Ross Carpenter writes, "Many an Ohio farm boy's introduction to China lay in digging ginseng, which he would sell for only pennies a pound.... He probably did not know that it was beginning a long journey that would end only when it was sold in an apothecary shop in China."[1] Ginseng was the primary cargo of the *Empress of China*, the first American ship to trade with China from an American point of departure, leaving from New York in 1784.[2] An earlier vessel, the *Harriet*, had left Boston in 1783 with the intention of sailing to Canton with its cargo of ginseng, but it exchanged its cargo early at the Cape of Good Hope for "double its weight in Hyson tea."[3]

The first American traders in China relied on ginseng and specie (essentially gold and silver coins) to obtain their valued cargoes of Chinese goods. They quickly determined that the market for and supply of ginseng were limited, and they could not rely on sparse stocks of gold and silver to maintain their trade. Given the lack of other goods available in the early republic, the logical recourse was to obtain goods outside the United States and then transport them to China to exchange for the Chinese tea, silk, and porcelain that would bring high prices on their return to their home ports.

Unfortunately, most of the commodities the American traders were able to procure outside the United States for the China trade had serious environmental consequences. Fur seal skins came to be the most successful commodity found during the time Lewis Coolidge was on the high seas, but the traders—not all of them Americans—devastated the populations of fur seals on nearly all the islands where they flourished before the advent of the China sealskin trade. Sandalwood, though not obtained and traded by the *Amethyst* during Lewis Coolidge's years aboard, was another prized commodity by the Chinese for its aroma. This tropical hardwood could be made into valuable scented boxes and was used in large construction such as temples. Sandalwood shavings were also burned as incense. A primary source of sandalwood was the forests of Hawaii, which were reduced to mere fractions of the original stands as local chiefs cut down their timber to exchange for armaments to be used in their inter-island wars. However, Carpenter notes that early sandalwood trade between American traders and Hawaiian chiefs (as well as whalers' visits and trade in fur seal skins) paved the way for the visits of missionaries and closer ties in other areas, which eventually led to a formal association with the United States.[4]

The fur seal trade was also instrumental in the acquisition of Alaska from Russia. The proximity of Alaska to China and the value of Alaskan seal pelts were pivotal influences in the narrow vote margin in Congress to complete the purchase agreement, sometimes known as "Seward's Folly" after Secretary of State William H. Seward, who negotiated the purchase.[5]

Bêche-de-mer or sea cucumbers sometimes referred as "trepang," was one commodity that the crew of the *Amethyst* was able to acquire in large quantities in the Palau Islands for sale to the Chinese who considered these sluglike creatures a delicacy in Chinese soups and other dishes. Lewis Coolidge dedicated approximately one-fourth of his entire journal to his time (January 26, 1810–June 3, 1810) in Palau (or "Pelew," as he referred to these islands), when he had particular responsibilities in obtaining a full cargo of bêche-de-mer. In their 1925 work on early American trade with the Orient, *Gold of Ophir*, Sydney and Marjorie Greenbie describe this bêche-de-mer trade as follows:

> Beche-de-mer (or sea-cucumber as it was called because of its shape), like sandalwood, was in great demand at Canton. This little creature is from six to fifteen inches long and lives on the coral reefs. Sometimes it has prickles on it, sometimes teats, and sometimes it is smooth. It is a very important part of Chinese diet, the process of curing being by boiling it for twenty minutes, then drying it in the sun. Later, it is smoked over a fire. When cooked in soups it is most agreeable and nourishing. The favourite variety is the "brown with teats," but the other four kinds—large black, small black, red-bellied, and white—are also edible. The brown-teat fish or slug fetches even today as much as $1,200 or more a ton.[6]

Sea cucumber, or bêche-de-mer. Specimen shown is the highly prized *Holothuria Scabra*. Courtesy of David Pawson, Smithsonian Institution

Another source describes the method of curing as follows: "Bêche-de-mer had to be cured by boiling in pothouses on shore, then dried and stored away in matting bags."[7]

Bêche-de-mer is still harvested in parts of Indonesia and other Pacific Island countries. According to David Pawson, a senior research scientist at the

National Museum of Natural History of the Smithsonian Institution, there has been a very active and far-flung fishery for sea cucumbers for at least the past thousand years—indeed, the fishery is as active today as it has ever been, with high-quality sea cucumber selling in markets in Hong Kong and Singapore for more than $100 per pound.[8] Dr. Pawson added that the commercially useful species of sea cucumbers are usually widespread, but the traffic in bêche-de-mer has caused local extinctions for extended periods of time through overfishing in a single area. Some species are reduced in numbers to the extent that there is some discussion of listing them as an endangered species with the Conference on International Trade in Endangered Species (CITES). (See photo on page 69 of one current species of sea cucumber.)

Lewis Coolidge and the rest of the crew of the *Amethyst* may have engaged in trade that had environmental downsides, but at least they avoided the reprehensible trade in opium. In the eighteenth century, the British had been sending opium legally from India to China for decades to pay for their return cargoes of tea until the Chinese banned the opium trade in 1800. Smuggling and bribing officials allowed the trade to continue. The first record of an American ship carrying opium into Canton was the *Eutaw* in 1806. The odious trade flourished—with Americans participating—until a few years after the end of the First Opium War around 1839 when the Chinese appointed a governor who would enforce China's prohibitions against the opium trade. The treaties ending the Opium War finally stopped most of the trade in the drug, but China ended up paying reparations for the opium it destroyed. The most far-reaching results of the treaties ending the Opium War were in opening up Chinese foreign trade—other ports aside from Canton could then engage in trade with foreigners, so there was no longer a set group of Chinese who could barter deals with foreigners. The Opium War thus ended the period known as the "Old China Trade."

| Fur Seals

Regardless of the importance of ginseng, sandalwood, bêche-de-mer, and other products, far and away the most significant product the Chinese received in trade from the Americans, except for specie, was fur seal skins.[9] The great majority of the trade was conducted within a generation but in that period of years, the traders virtually wiped out the fur seal populations on many barren outposts in the Southern Hemisphere. The only substantial rookeries remaining were in the Northern Hemisphere, centered around the Pribilof Islands in Alaska.

Fur seals and other seals, sea lions, and walruses are members of the super-family *Pinnipedia,* meaning they have "fins or wing-like structures (pinni) for feet (ped)."[10] The superfamily *Pinnipedia* is composed of three families:

Otariidae: "Eared" seals—fur seals and sea lions. These seals have visible ears and are generally referred to as eared seals. A further distinction is that their hind flippers are large relative to their entire body structure and can be rotated up under their bodies so that they can essentially walk on their four flippers. Thus, the seals in circuses and water shows are otariids, usually sea lions. The fur of fur seals is attractive and thick and retains its water-repellant characteristics when made into hats, coats, and the like. One of the most popu-lar items of apparel in the nineteenth century was the fur seal sacque—a loose wrap, cloak, or cape.

Phocidae: "True" seals—monk seals, hair seals, elephant seals, and so on. True seals have no ears on the outsides of their heads. Their hind flippers can-not be rotated up under their bodies so that they can only move on land by wiggling and sliding. The white baby harp seals that have been the subject of controversial hunts by Canadian trappers in recent years are not fur seals but rather hair seals, phocids. With the exception of the baby harp seals, phocids have not been hunted for their fur, which is brittle and less pliable than that of fur seals. Populations of elephant seals were drastically reduced in the nine-teenth century as hunters sought their blubber to convert to oil similar to the hunting of whales for whale oil.

Odobenidae: These are walruses, the familiar large marine mammals with long tusks. Males are often ten feet long and weigh over a ton. Their ivory tusks attracted hunters who also used walruses as a source of oil.

Until the beginning of large-scale fur sealing at the end of the eighteenth century and the early to mid–nineteenth century, fur seals were found in vast numbers in some of the least accessible parts of the world, particularly on the islands of the extreme southern hemisphere. The map showing the route of the *Amethyst* demonstrates the distribution and prevalence of fur seals in the far southern waters (page xx). Antarctica, the Antarctic islands, and the southern-most part of the South American mainland—Tierra del Fuego and Patagonia—were fertile grounds. Islands with significant rookeries in this area near South America included San Félix and Juan Fernández Islands off the coast of Chile (in particular Más Afuera, now known as Alejandro Selkirk Island in the Juan Fernández group), the Falkland Islands, and the Galapagos Islands. Fur seal islands close to Antarctica include South Georgia Island and the South Sandwich group, the South Orkneys, the South Shetlands, the Auckland

Islands, and Campbell Island; in short, nearly every island off the Antarctic coast. Closer to the Cape of Good Hope, there were significant rookeries on Gough Island, Bouvet Island, Prince Edward Island, Marion Island, the Crozette group, the Kerguelen Islands, and Tristan da Cunha, particularly "Little Nightingale."

In the northern hemisphere, there were far fewer good sites for fur seal rookeries with the appropriate conditions for landing and breeding grounds: the union of cool water, well-adapted landings, and moist, foggy air. There were virtually no significant rookeries in the North Atlantic. Far and away the largest concentrations in the northern hemisphere were found in the Pacific in the Pribilof and Commander Islands in the Bering Sea. Several islands off Southern California and Mexico, including Santa Catalina and Guadeloupe, were also sites with great populations, which were hunted extensively. Lewis Coolidge spent a year on the San Benito Islands just off California harvesting seals, while the *Amethyst* sailed thousands of miles, returning back east around the Horn, then to Gough Island near the Cape of Good Hope, then back west past the Horn, on to Australia, and finally back east across the Pacific to pick up Coolidge in May 1808.

The "Old China Trade" in fur skins reportedly began in 1778 on the final voyage of the ship of English explorer Captain James Cook.[11] In 1775, Cook discovered the island of South Georgia and recorded the quality of the fur seals on that island. Later, Cook had acquired fur skins, likely sea otters, in trade with Indians on the northwestern coast of North America. Captain Cook did not complete the voyage on to Canton, as he was killed by Hawaiians when his vessel stopped there later in that voyage. The ship, however, continued without him on to Canton, where the Chinese spotted the furs somewhat by accident and offered relatively great sums ($50 apiece) for them. A young American marine, John Ledyard, was on board that ship and remembered the Chinese interest in the skins. Ledyard spent the rest of his life trying unsuccessfully to develop this trade, reportedly meeting with Thomas Jefferson in France. While Ledyard was not able to make a fortune in the China fur trade, his efforts led others to buy sea otter skins in the American Northwest and to send them to Canton. The first recorded American ship voyage engaged in this early trade in sea otter furs occurred in 1788 by the *Columbia*, which sailed down the great river in the current state of Washington, a river that came to bear the ship's name. Carpenter includes the *Amethyst* among the ships engaged in this early trade long before Lewis Coolidge shipped aboard. Carpenter also mentions Captain Ebenezer Dorr, patriarch of the Dorr family that owned the *Amethyst* on Lewis Coolidge's voyage, as likely the first American captain to poach furskins illegally off the Spanish California coast on his ship the *Otter* around 1796.[12] When the sea otters became scarce, the trappers turned to fur seals.

Seals had been taken for their fur by Aleuts, Fuegians, and other indigenous peoples for centuries, and the Russians began taking and trading fur seal skins shortly after the early voyages of Vitus Bering, beginning in 1728, in the sea that bears his name. Later, the Russian trading companies began extensive exploitation of the large seal rookeries of the Commander Islands (1741) and the Pribilofs (1786), the latter named after a Russian trading company navigator, Gerassim Pribilof. As noted earlier, the commercial significance of Southern Hemisphere seals was recorded in Capt. Cook's published journal in his discovery of South Georgia in 1775. About the same time, there were records of ongoing sealing in New Amsterdam in the southern Indian Ocean and the Falklands near Argentina in the southern Atlantic.[13]

The first record of an American ship engaged in the Old China Trade in fur seal skins came in 1786 when the *United States* out of Boston delivered 13,000 fur seal skins to its home port and then transshipped them on to Canton in the *Eleonora*.[14] In Canton, the seal skins brought the fine price of five dollars each, ten times the price they could fetch in the eastern United States.[15] After the success of the *United States,* other ships joined the market to bring much financial success to the American sailors and traders but devastation to the seal populations on their Southern Hemisphere islands. For example, Captain Amaso Delano estimated that from 1797 to 1804, three million sealskins were taken from the island of Más Afuera, now known as Alejandro Selkirk Island, in the Juan Fernández Archipelago off the coast of Chile. American exports of fur seal skins easily numbered in the hundreds of thousands in the first decade of the nineteenth century as 154 American ships registered in Canton between 1804 and 1809.[16]

As a matter of course, sealers took entire populations of seals without regard to leaving behind sufficient numbers to replenish the rookeries. The traders simply took all the seals they found. This rampant devastation took its toll in a relatively short period of time, and seal populations, particularly in the Southern Hemisphere, declined drastically. During the War of 1812, British interference with American shipping and the difficulty of finding seals combined to mark the end of the boom period in the Canton fur seal trade. The trade continued at lower levels for decades and then resurged for a time in the late 1800s. However, fur seal populations were down permanently, never to recover from the depredations of the sealers despite international treaties and other regulation in the twentieth century.

The War of 1812 disrupted not only the fur seal skin trade but all American trade worldwide. The China trade was affected as seriously as any. The British fleet controlled the Pacific from a few years before 1812 until peace was declared in the Treaty of Ghent, signed on Christmas Eve, 1815. Those British ships kept American ones off the northwest coast of what is now the United States and out of Hawaii.[17] There were even incidents in Canton Harbor. The HMSo *Doris* had captured the American vessel *Hunter* off the Ladrone Islands (now known as the Marianas) and took her to Canton. The *Doris* later attacked and captured an American schooner within ten miles of Canton.[18] When the open hostilities of the War of 1812 began, the British initiated a blockade of Canton Harbor, which kept American ships out of the trade until peace came at the end of 1815. Because of this interference with shipping, the total U.S.-China trade for the period 1812 to 1815 amounted to barely half the trade in 1811 alone and only a third of overall U.S. trade for the period 1809 to 1811.[19]

The Treaty of Ghent, signed on December 24, 1814, that concluded the War of 1812 and the second Peace of Paris on November 20, 1815, that ended the Napoleonic Wars between France and Britain revitalized U.S.-China trade. The wars had disrupted the worldwide trade in Chinese goods and brought high prices for Chinese tea and silk. A significant percentage of this trade was carried in American bottoms for reshipment to Europe. As the fur trade began to decline because of the declining populations of fur seals, specie began to become an overwhelming percentage of U.S. exports. From 1816 to 1820, American exports to China amounted to $33,930,107, of which $25,779,000 were specie and bullion, nearly 76 percent. After 1826, specie came to be replaced with bills of exchange on England, the basic debt instrument in use at the time. American cotton goods gradually became an important export after the War of 1812. Other exports included ginseng, quicksilver, copper, lead, rice, and steel; all but ginseng were sourced outside the United States. U.S. trade with China in opium was significant but it was only a small percentage of the British trade. Since this trade was contraband, no reliable statistics are available, but Shü-Lun Pon in his *Trade of the United States with China*, notes a reference to one source estimating that from 1827 to 1830, Americans brought 160,000 to 190,000 pounds of opium into China annually.[20] When opium was surrendered to the Chinese in 1839 in the process ending the Opium War, Americans surrendered a total of 1,540 chests out of a total of 20,283, mainly from the British side. Thomas Layton also notes a reference that Americans controlled about 10 percent of the Chinese opium trade.[21]

In the years immediately prior to the War of 1812, American imports from China were roughly three to six million dollars per year. The large majority of

U.S. exports to China were in the form of specie (gold and silver coins and bullion) in spite of the American traders' efforts at finding suitable commodities such as fur skins, sandalwood, bêche-de-mer, ginseng, and so on. For the entire 1805–1815 period, U.S. exports of specie to China amounted to approximately $22.7 million, or approximately 70 percent of the total.[22]

Trade with China was very important to the United States right after the American Revolution because of the paucity of available trading partners. Products available in China, particularly tea and porcelain, were important to the citizens of the new republic. However, the "Old China Trade" has remained controversial because of the environmental consequences of the exports of products like fur seal skins, sea cucumbers, and sandalwood and the social consequences of the opium trade.

3
The Lewis Coolidge Family

Lewis Coolidge was born in Boston, Massachusetts, on September 16, 1783. He was a fifth-generation descendant of John and Mary Coolidge, who emigrated from England in 1630 and settled in Watertown, Massachusetts.[1] Prior to emigration, John and Mary had lived in the small village of Cottenham, which, while relatively remote from London, was nevertheless later described as "seething under a turmoil of religious, political and financial contention."[2] The political trauma affecting central England had also reached Cottenham; by 1630, King Charles I had already dismissed Parliament three times. Cottenham was likely affected more than other similar villages, as it is recorded that Oliver Cromwell frequently stayed at its rectory.[3] John and Mary Coolidge were doubtless affected by the fever of the times and, further, were likely religious dissenters as they were married in a civil ceremony rather than in the church. John Coolidge's father had died in 1618 and his mother Margaret (Mayse) Coolidge in 1620. The family wealth had been divided among the heirs. There was little to keep John and Mary in Cottenham, and emigration to the new world became an appealing alternative to the religious and civil discomfort that John and Mary must have felt in England. The Coolidges are not listed in any of the passenger lists, but Emma Downing Coolidge writes that "there is little doubt that they sailed in the Company that accompanied the new Governor, John Winthrop, to Massachusetts Bay."[4] This was the "Winthrop Fleet" of eleven ships that brought about seven hundred Puritans to New England in 1630.

In Watertown, John Coolidge's name is regularly listed among the town's most senior citizens. Watertown at that time extended well beyond the current town boundaries and encompassed the present-day towns of Dedham, Sudbury, Weston, Belmont, Waltham, and part of Cambridge.[5] John Coolidge was admitted as a "freeman" in 1636 and elected "selectman" in 1638, a position he held for nearly forty years.[6] In 1658, John Coolidge served as deputy to the

Great and General Court of Massachusetts Bay. Further, his name is recorded numerous times on town committees, settling land disputes, inventorying estates, and drawing up wills. He died in Watertown in 1691 at the age of 88; Mary died just four months later, also at the age of 88.

John and Mary Coolidge had eight children. Lewis Coolidge was descended from the youngest, Jonathan, who became head of the Boston branch of the family. President Calvin Coolidge was descended from the third child and second son, Simon. The Watertown estate of John and Mary Coolidge was willed to the sixth child, Stephen, who, childless, was taken care of in his old age by two of Jonathan's daughters, Mary and Martha Coolidge. Jonathan married Martha Rice in 1679, the granddaughter of Edmund Rice, a distinguished citizen of Sudbury who held various civic positions in the town, including selectman, deacon, justice of the peace, and member of the General Court.[7] Jonathan himself was active in civic affairs; as surveyor, he surveyed many of the highways and other landmarks around Watertown.

Of Jonathan and Martha's seven children, John was the fifth, named after his grandfather, and he was the great-grandfather of Lewis Coolidge. John was born at Watertown but spent his entire life in Boston, marrying Hannah Ingram there in 1713. John and Hannah had thirteen children; the fourth was Joseph, who in 1746 married a French Huguenot, Marguerite Olivier. Marguerite was born in Nova Scotia, the daughter of Anthoine Olivier who had crossed the Atlantic with his Sigourney and Germaine relatives after the revocation of the Edict of Nantes in 1685. The Edict of Nantes had given basic religious rights to Protestants in France, and its revocation marked an ominous turn. Anthoine Olivier and his group landed first in Boston but then moved to Annapolis, Nova Scotia, for several years, returning then to Boston.

Joseph and Marguerite had eight children, three of whom died as infants or small children. Of the remaining five, most played roles in the Revolution. The eldest child, Joseph, was a Son of Liberty and one of the "Indians" at the Boston Tea Party. Joseph later founded a successful import trading company. Mary, the sixth child, married Zachariah Hicks who was the son of John Hicks, said to be the first man killed by British troops on April 19, 1775, at the Battle of Lexington.[8]

Lieut. John Coolidge, the third child and the father of Lewis Coolidge, was married to Lydia Dawes, the sister of William "Billy" Dawes who rode with Paul Revere. Both Billy Dawes and John Coolidge were "warm friend[s] and helper[s] of Dr. Joseph Warren," the Son of Liberty who drafted the Suffolk Resolves of September 9, 1774, which "declared the British Coercive Acts to be unconstitutional and void, urged Massachusetts to form a free state until and unless they were repealed, advised the people to arm themselves, and recommended economic sanctions against Britain."[9] Billy Dawes's father, William Dawes Sr, was limited in physical participation in the Revolution by his club-foot, but he was known for support of its causes and sent the apprentices from his tailor shop to pretend to be Indians at the Boston Tea Party along with Joseph Coolidge. As noted in Holland's book on Dawes, The elder William Dawes's "apprentices were among the party who threw the tea overboard in Boston Harbor. The daughters of the family sat up for them; and when they came in, the rims of their hats, which were turned up a little, were loaded with tea, which the young women vigorously shook into the fire, while they listened to the story of what was then thought a daring but boyish escapade."[10] Billy Dawes's first cousin, Thomas Dawes, Jr., son of the brother of William Dawes Sr., was another well-known patriot. He was a member of various Boston committees along with Samuel Adams and John Hancock. As John Adams wrote in his diary in February 1763,

> This day learned that the Caucus Club meets, at certain times, in the garret of Tom Dawes.... There they smoke tobacco till you cannot see from one end of the garret to the other. There they drink flip, I suppose, and there they choose ... selectmen, assessors, collectors, wardens, firewards and representatives are regularly chosen before they are chosen in the town. Uncle Fairfield, Story, Ruddock, [Sam] Adams, Cooper, and a rudis indigestaque moles of others are members. They send committees to wait on the merchants' club, and to propose and join in the choice of men and measures. Captain Cunningham says they have solicited him to go to these caucuses; they have assured him of benefit in his business.[11]

The Caucus Club was one of the early organizations for self-determination that gave rise to such entities as the Committees of Correspondence advocating revolution.

John Coolidge took an active military role in the Revolution as a member of Capt. J. Stoddard's Company from 1776–1777. He fought in the Battle of Bunker Hill and was commissioned there as a second lieutenant. At Bunker Hill, his longtime colleague, now Gen. Peter Warren, met his untimely death, which was immortalized in John Trumbull's painting, "The Death of Warren." It is not known whether any of the figures depicted in Trumbull's painting were intended to represent John Coolidge.

After the midnight rides by Paul Revere, Billy Dawes, and Dr. Samuel Prescott on April 18, 1775, and the subsequent battles of Lexington, Concord, and Bunker Hill, the British imposed a siege on Boston and began to conduct

Portrait of William Dawes, Jr. (1745–1799). This is the Billy Dawes who rode with Paul Revere. Artist believed to be John Johnston. Courtesy of the Evanston Historical Society, Evanston, Illinois

house-to-house searches for known revolutionaries. Since both Billy Dawes and John Coolidge were in that category, they fled Boston with their families and went into a joint grocery business in Worcester, Massachusetts, about fifty miles west of Boston.[12] John Coolidge subsequently became a lieutenant in the Light Infantry Company of the Boston militia in 1779.

After the war John Coolidge returned to Boston and opened a grocery store with his brother-in-law Billy Dawes in Dock Square.[13] Since 1778, Coolidge had owned what was known as the Jackson mansion nearby on Sudbury Street, owned by Samuel Jackson until his death in that year. Samuel Jackson was the father of William Dawes Sr.'s second wife, Hannah. Upon Jackson's death, William and Hannah and the other heirs sold the house to John Coolidge for £1,200.[14]

The next generation of Coolidges—particularly the children of John Coolidge and his brother Joseph—took part in the burgeoning field of international trade that helped spur growth in the fledgling republic. John and Lydia Coolidge's daughter, Lydia, married Eben Farley who was a member of the "well-known firm of Boston merchants, Swett and Farley."[15] Lewis Coolidge was a clerk at Swett and Farley until the age of 22 when he went to sea aboard the *Amethyst*. Lewis's brother, William Coolidge, became a merchant in Boston and then later in Baltimore. William's son John Pannell Coolidge, Lewis's nephew, was "second officer on board a Boston East Indiamen."[16]

Joseph Coolidge II, brother of Lieut. John Coolidge and uncle to Lewis Coolidge, who had been one of the Sons of Liberty and one of the "Indians" at the Boston Tea Party, set up a business importing goods, particularly wine, from Great Britain. His son, Joseph Coolidge III, inherited and expanded his father's established business. Joseph III, married his second cousin, Elizabeth Bulfinch, who was the sister of Charles Bulfinch, architect and one of the financiers of the *Columbia*, the first American vessel engaged in the Pacific sea otter fur trade, in what is now the American Northwest. The *Columbia* gave its name to the river sailed on this epic voyage located in what is today Washington State.[17] A nephew of Elizabeth Bulfinch Coolidge, Thomas Bulfinch, wrote the classic *Bulfinch's Mythology*, and numerous other books.

Joseph Coolidge IV, Lewis Coolidge's first cousin once removed, was a well-known China trader. While still in his formative years, he traveled widely and made the acquaintance of the writers Washington Irving and Lord Byron. On July 5, 1821, Lord Byron wrote to Thomas Moore from Ravenna:

> I have had a friend of your Mr. [Washington] Irving's—a very pretty lad—a Mr. Coolidge of Boston—only somewhat too full of poesy and "entussymussy." I was very civil to him during his few hours' stay, and talked with him much of Irving, whose writings are my delight. But I suspect that he did not take quite so much to me, from his having expected to meet a misanthropical gentleman, in wolfskin breeches, and answering in fierce monosyllables, instead of a man of this world.[18]

In number 25 of his Detached Thoughts, Lord Byron wrote:

> A young American, named Coolidge, called on me not many months ago: he was intelligent, very handsome, and not more than twenty years old according to appearances. A little romantic, but that sits well upon youth, and mighty fond of poesy as may be suspected from his approaching me in my cavern. He brought me a message from an old Servant of my family [Joe Murray] and told me that he [Mr. Coolidge] had obtained a copy of my bust from Thorwaldsen in Rome to send to America. I confess I was more flattered by this young enthusiasm in a solitary trans-Atlantic traveller, than if they had decreed me a Statue in the Paris Pantheon.... I say I was more flattered by it because it was single, unpolitical, and was without motive or ostentation—the pure and warm feeling of a boy for the poet he admired. It must have been expensive though, I would not pay

Portrait of
Joseph Coolidge IV
(1798–1879). By Alfred L.
Smith. Courtesy of
Harvard University,
Portrait Collection, Gift
of Joseph Randolph
Coolidge, 1981

the price of a Thorwaldsen bust for any human head and shoulders, except Napoleon's, or my children's, or some "absurd Womankind's" as Monkbarns calls them, or my Sister's.[19]

After Joseph Coolidge IV returned from Europe, he traveled in Virginia, where he met (and courted) Eleanora Wayles Randolph, the granddaughter of Thomas Jefferson. The two were married May 27, 1825. Joseph's first business experience was in a joint venture with his first cousin, Thomas Bulfinch, from 1825 to 1832 as "American goods commission merchants." At that point, Joseph left to begin his lengthy China work as a clerk for Russell and Company in Canton, while his cousin Thomas Bulfinch turned to his life's work writing such books as *Bulfinch's Mythology*, *The Age of Fable*, and *The Age of Chivalry*. In 1834, Joseph Coolidge returned from China and became a partner in Russell and Company. He then returned to China and spent most of the next few years there as well as some time in India. In 1840, he left Russell and Company and was one of the founders of the trading company of Augustine Heard and Company, which had China as its focus. With the outbreak of the Opium War between China and Britain shortly after the founding of Augustine Heard and Co., British subjects fled Canton, and with Joseph Coolidge IV as its principal

Canton representative, Augustine Heard and Co. became the Canton agent of the giant English trader Jardine, Matheson, and Company.

In 1844 Joseph left China and retired on his earnings from his China trade. His family continued in international trade. His sister Elizabeth Boyer Coolidge married Tasker Hazard Swett, a partner in the Boston Trading Company of Swett and Farley where Lewis Coolidge had labored as a clerk before going to sea on the *Amethyst.*

Joseph's son Sydney was a scientist who served as the astronomer on Commodore Perry's expedition to Japan but was killed in action at the Battle of Chickamauga during the Civil War in 1863. Joseph's son, Thomas Jefferson Coolidge, was president of various manufacturing, transportation, and financial enterprises including the Atchison, Topeka, and Santa Fe railroads. Joseph's grandson, Thomas Jefferson Coolidge, Jr., was an executive of several major financial enterprises such as the Old Colony Trust Company and the First National Bank of Boston. Later, he became the chairman of the board of the United Fruit Company.

As noted earlier, President Calvin Coolidge was descended from Simon, third child of the emigrating ancestors John and Mary Coolidge of Watertown, Massachusetts, while Lewis Coolidge was descended from John and Mary's eighth child, Jonathan. That makes Lewis and Calvin fourth cousins,

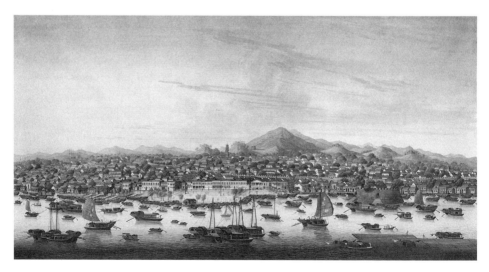

The wharf at Canton, circa 1820. Courtesy of the
Peabody Essex Museum, Salem, Massachusetts

four times removed. Lewis was actually a much closer relative of President Calvin Coolidge's running mate Charles Dawes, who was a direct descendant of Lewis's uncle, Billy Dawes. Charles Dawes and Lewis Coolidge were first cousins, three times removed.

John Coolidge (1603–1691)

Simon (1632–1693)   Jonathan (1646–1723)
Obadiah, I (1663–1706)   John (1690–?)
Obadiah, II (1695–1739)   Joseph (1718–1746)
Josiah (1718–1780)   John (1750–1815)
John (1756–1822)   Lewis Coolidge (1783–1872)
Calvin (1780–1853)
Calvin Galusha (1815–1878)
John Calvin (1845–1926)
President Calvin Coolidge (1872–1933)
William Dawes (1620–1703)
Ambros (1642–1705)
Thomas (1680–1750)
William, Sr. (1719–1802)

William Dawes, Sr. (1719–1800)

William, Jr. (1745–1799)   Lydia (1747–1815)
William Mears (1771–1855)   Lewis Coolidge (1783–1872)
Henry (1804–1867)
Rufus Republic (1838–1899)
Vice-President Charles Gates Dawes (1865–1951)

Coolidge-Dawes
campaign button

Photograph of the Coolidge reunion, circa 1935–40.
Front row: John Felt, Maxine Felt, Alice Louise Coolidge McMullen, Clifton McMullen. *Seated:* Adelaide Coolidge Felt, [unidentified], Sue Coolidge (holding Carol Grant), Shirley Grant, Emily Coolidge McCoy holding Patricia Grant, Bob Grant, Addie Humes. *Standing:* Dan McCoy, Winifred McCoy, Jane McCoy, Aunt Nell (Eleanor Coolidge), Bert Coolidge, [unidentified], [unidentified], Harley Felt, Lan McClellan, Arthur Humes

| Lewis Coolidge after the *Amethyst's* Voyage

Lewis Coolidge returned to the United States on the *Amethyst* on April 3, 1811. He soon went back to the sea in another merchantman, the *Volant*, out of Boston, under Nathaniel Perley, master. Coolidge's seafaring life continued to be plagued by misfortune. The following is an account of the vessel's 1812–1813 voyage contained in a Perley genealogy:[21]

> They sailed from Boston on the 28th of March of that year [1812]. The vessel arrived at Bayonne, France, with her cargo, in safety. On the 16th of April, the outward cargo was completely discharged, and on the same day Capt. Perley commenced loading with brandy for a return cargo. On the 18th of May they had laden on board four hundred pipes of brandy.[20] The ship was detained from this time till the middle of September, waiting for a license from the Emperor to depart with the cargo. The license being obtained, the ship was ready to sail on the last day of September, but was detained by adverse winds and tides until the fifth of November,

when she sailed from Bayonne bound for Boston. In attempting to go to sea the vessel struck the bar, which obliged the captain to take out part of the cargo, and to return to Bayonne for repairs. They were again detained by the repairs and unfavorable winds and tides until the 12th of February, 1813, when they again set sail for Boston. On the 26th of March following, the ship was captured by a British war vessel, and sent to Halifax, where she was afterwards condemned, with her whole cargo, which were wholly lost to the owners.

The British war vessel that captured the *Volant* was the *Curlew,* an eighteen-gun *Cruizer*-class brig-sloop under the command of Michael Head. "On 26 March 1813 Capt. Head captured the American privateer Volante [*sic*], pierced for 22 guns but mounting ten 24 pounder canonnades and four long 9 pounders."[22] The *Volant,* given its armament, was described in the above account as a privateer rather than a merchantman. However, in his history of privateering in the War of 1812, George Coggeshall lists the *Volant* as a "letter-of-marque" rather than as a "privateer," with the distinction that a privateer was implied to be a licensed raider that did not trade.[23] A letter-of-marque would raid and trade. This distinction was often blurred, with letters-of-marque included in the broad category of privateers. The Perley genealogy referenced above describes Capt. Perley as "an intrepid privateersman and delighted to play mischief with the Red-coats."[24]

Privateers constituted a significant arm of the American war effort in the War of 1812. At the start of the War of 1812, the British Royal Navy had 584 ships in full commission, the mightiest maritime power in the world. Samuel Eliot Morison notes that "526 privateers were fitted out from the United States but this doubtless includes letter-of-marque vessels which were primarily traders, not commerce destroyers."[25] This figure dwarfed the number of U.S. Navy vessels: 8 frigates, 12 sloops, and odd small craft for duties on the Great Lakes.[26] Morison further notes that "privateering was much the most popular form of service in maritime Massachusetts; it paid better wages, was safer, and more fun than the army or navy."[27] Stephen Howarth makes a similar observation in his history of the U.S. Navy: "Privateering was much more popular than naval service: It was more profitable, less risky, less dsciplined, just as exciting, and everyone had the necessary sea skills already."[28]

Lewis Coolidge may have enjoyed his time aboard a privateer before the *Volant's* capture by the *Curlew,* but certainly not after that point. He was taken prisoner and held for eighty-four days in Halifax, Nova Scotia.[29] During that imprisonment, according to his own account in a publication of the Old Settlers

Union of Peoria County, Illinois, "John Bull's commons of pea soup and middlings had reduced me to an anatomy of a tailor's yard."[30] After his release he remained incensed by his treatment by the British and enlisted as a private in Lieut. Col. P. Osgood's Second Regiment of the Massachusetts Militia, in a company led by Captain Jonathan Whitney, which operated near Boston at that time. Coolidge was called upon to serve only thirty days of active duty in that unit (July 1–30, 1814).[31]

After he left the army, Lewis Coolidge moved to Waltham, Vermont, between the Green Mountains and Lake Champlain, where he took up teaching and farming. On December 13, 1818, he married Amanda Mills Dennison, the daughter of Christopher Dennison, Jr., an Addison County farmer and, like Lewis, a War of 1812 veteran. Christopher Dennison, Sr. was a Revolutionary War veteran and a direct descendant of Mayflower passengers John Howland, John Tilley, and Elizabeth Tilley. At the time of their marriage, Lewis was thirty-three years old, and Amanda was sixteen. As H. P. Smith notes, "The farm now owned by J. and E. J. Hurlburt was first occupied by Christopher Dennison, Jr. It soon passed to the ownership of Lewis Coolidge, from Boston, Mass. He was a good citizen, but never a practical farmer. He occupied the farm some fifteen years, then sold the same to Philemon Alvord."[32] Smith also observes that "the so-called Bacon farm is the same that was early occupied by Christopher Dennison, Jr., the first representative elected from this town."[33] Five of the six children of Lewis and Amanda were born in Waltham; three died in childhood. Surviving were Edward Lewis, born in 1825, and Ellen Jeannette, born in 1832. After twenty years in Vermont, Lewis Coolidge became interested in lands to the west. As a veteran of the War of 1812, he was eligible for a land warrant to property in the Military Tract, the large expanse of land in Illinois, bounded generally by the Rock River, the Illinois River, and the Mississippi River. No land warrant or bounty has been found for Lewis Coolidge, but he obtained rights to land in Peoria County, Illinois, most likely through outright purchase. In 1834, Lewis, Amanda, Edward, and Ellen moved west to the community of Willow Brook, near Kickapoo, Peoria County, about fifteen miles northwest of the center of present-day Peoria, Illinois. In 1836, Lewis and Amanda's last child, Emily Dennison, was born in their new Illinois home.

The Coolidge property was on wooded, hilly land. It was difficult to clear and then difficult to raise crops. However, it was on the stage route from Pekin to the Mississippi River. Around 1840, Lewis converted part of his house into a tavern to feed and house passengers from the stage line. In 1835, another settler moved into reasonable proximity of Coolidge's farm, only about a mile from his settlement. Philander Chase, the founder of Kenyon College in Ohio and

Jubilee College Chapel. Lithograph by Charles Overall.
Courtesy of Jubilee State Park

Jubilee College Chapel as it appeared in 2006. Photograph by J. Felt

the newly appointed Episcopal Bishop for the Illinois Diocese, had selected land near Lewis Coolidge to build Jubilee College to train Episcopal priests for the frontier. Chase was the uncle and guardian of Salmon Chase, who went on to become secretary of the Treasury in the Abraham Lincoln administration and then chief justice of the United States Supreme Court.

Philander Chase raised a significant amount of funds in the eastern and southern states and in England to support Jubilee College. He built a two-story Gothic Revival building as a combination chapel, classroom area, and dormitory as well as several other buildings. In 1840, Jubilee College opened with a theological department, a college for men, a preparatory school for boys, and a girls' school. The college was so attractive that Lewis Coolidge had the trees topped between his home and the college so he could gaze on it in the evening light. Coolidge and Bishop Chase reportedly enjoyed many thoughtful conversations, and Lewis eventually forsook his New England religion for Bishop Chase's Episcopalianism. Chase died in 1852, and his brother, Samuel, took over management of the school. Unfortunately the dependency on donations from southern states would prove fatal when that source dried up during the Civil War, eventually leading the college to close its doors in 1862. The two-story stone chapel building remains as the "centerpiece of a ninety-acre state historic site managed by the Illinois Historic Preservation Agency."[34]

The area around Lewis Coolidge's home, "Willow Brook," was often called "Robin's Nest," the name that Bishop Chase bestowed on his own home. More often, though, it was referred to as "the Coolidge Settlement." In 1837, the Peoria area was developing, thanks in great part to the ending of the Blackhawk War and the Land Act of 1812 (with significant underpinning from the Land Ordinance of 1785 and the Land Act of 1796), which opened the Military Tract for land warrants for War of 1812 veterans and for general land sales.[35] By the mid-1830s, a newspaper, the *Peoria Register and North-Western Gazetteer,* was well established under the guidance of its publisher and editor, Samuel H. Davis, who asked Lewis Coolidge for a writeup on the community known as the Coolidge Settlement. In Coolidge's short letter, published in the December 2, 1837, edition of the newspaper, he described the countryside around Willow Brook in glowing terms. He wrote, "The graceful undulations of the marginal hills and bluffs of 'red bud,' the richness of the woods, the solemnity of its shady knolls, and the deep repose that pervades the same."[36] He was ebullient about the prospects for the community, given the recent influx of settlers and the progress in the building of Jubilee College. The optimism that Lewis Coolidge expressed in his piece in the *Peoria Register and North-West Gazetteer* in 1837 faded over the next decade. In 1843, in a letter to his nephew, Charles

The twelve children of Edward Coolidge and Molly Palmer.
Standing: Bert Coolidge, Emily McCoy, Julia Hayward, Carrie Chapin,
Jennie Meehan, John Coolidge. *Seated:* Harry Coolidge, Eleanor (Nell) Coolidge,
Mabel Knight, Kate Beeson, Ben Coolidge. *In front:* Nancy Adelaide Coolidge Felt

Dawes Coolidge, in Boston, he wrote of the economic hardships faced by many farmers on the frontier. Bad weather took an entire wheat crop. Credit was almost nonexistent, and basic necessities such as clothing and paper were only available in poor quality at high prices.[37] (The text of Lewis Coolidge's newspaper piece and his 1843 letter to his nephew can be found as appendixes to this book.) In Coolidge's letter to his nephew, he mentioned that another nephew, Frank Dennison Farley, while visiting Lewis Coolidge, had bought some land in the Willow Brook area and then sold it at a great profit to Bishop Chase, since the land was a natural extension of Jubilee College. After a few years, Lewis Coolidge did the same. More land was available not far from Peoria, in the new community of Brimfield. He was able to purchase 240 acres of more productive land, which was to stay in the Coolidge family for more than a generation. As Lewis Coolidge's children grew to marrying age, Coolidge probably used to advantage his time and experience operating a tavern along the stage route near Pekin, Peoria, and Galesburg. One of the stage drivers that drove that route was Clarendon Palmer, who was born in Otsego County, New York, but moved to Galesburg, Illinois, around the time that Lewis Coolidge settled in Peoria County. Palmer and Coolidge may have discussed that they had children of similar ages. They may have also discussed common family interests in the sea and in the fur seal skin trade with China. Palmer's father was from Stonington, Connecticut, a major home port for sealers and China traders. Clarendon was a fourth cousin of Capt. Nathaniel B. Palmer, who was a well-known captain of several ships engaged in the China trade and in fur sealing. Capt. Palmer is also credited with discovering a long neck of Antarctica due south of Cape Horn; it is still known as Palmer Land.[38]

Clarendon Palmer died in 1852, but he had two children—a son Edwin, who married Ellen Coolidge, and a daughter Mary Ellen, called "Molly," who married Edward Coolidge. Lewis and Amanda's only other child, Emily, married Samuel Goodwin from nearby Elmwood, Illinois. Edwin and Molly Coolidge raised twelve children on the 240 acres that Lewis Coolidge had bought in the 1850s. Emily and Samuel Goodwin farmed nearby in Elmwood. Edward Palmer became a railroad engineer and later owned and operated an iron manufacturing plant in Richmond, Indiana. Lewis Coolidge's beloved wife, Amanda, died in 1858 and Lewis outlived her by fourteen years, passing away in 1872. Both died in Brimfield, Illinois, but they chose as their burial site the grounds of the beautiful Jubilee College that Lewis so admired.

APPENDIX A

Lewis Coolidge's Letter to the Editor of the *Peoria Register and North-Western Gazetteer*, December 2, 1837

Written for the *Peoria Register and North-Western Gazetteer*
December 2, 1837

THE COOLIDGE SETTLEMENT

Mr. Davis: Agreeably to your request, you have herewith a list of this settlement, comprising a circuit of three miles. It would be difficult at this time to ascertain the particular period of each family's arrival. I presume it sufficient to say, that little more than three years since, there were but two families in the precinct, since which, but mostly during the last year, the settlement have arrived to its present number, unprecedented, I believe, by any other in the county.

With much deference and respect, I have introduced the venerated name of the Rt. Rev. bishop of the diocese of this state and sincerely join the intelligent part of the community in the devout hope, that the college he contemplates erecting, may ere long, rear its graceful turrets over the romantic banks of the Kickapoo, and prove the alma mater of this and future generations! The graceful undulations of the marginal hills and bluffs of "red bud," the richness of the woods, the solemnity of its shady knolls, and the deep repose that pervades the same, are circumstances which, under the vicinity of "Robin's Nest," the most interesting and perhaps the most beautiful of any in the country, and peculiarly adapted as the site of a literary institution. The very valuable acquisition of two medical gentlemen has been made during the last year, whose reputation in their vocation is fully established. Indeed sir, we have every reason to be grateful and contented and believe, I do not know of any settler who thinks it 'expedient' to leave Kickapoo, the home of his adoption. Suffer me to add, that the stranger will realize an exquisite delight in the beauty of its scenery, and a reconciling view of human nature, in the intelligence, integrity and friendly disposition of the inhabitants.

Yours, &c.

L. Coolidge
From New England
Rt. Rev. Bishop Chase
Rev. Samuel Chase
Benjamin Miller
Hiram Chapman
Joseph Chapman
Benjamin Jacobs
Benjamin Rodgers
Austin Wood
Cyrus Wood
Lewis Taylor
Charles Chapman
John Chapman
William L Moss
Cyrus Tucker
Frank D. Farley
Harry H. Dennison
Lewis Coolidge
Virginia
John Combs, Esq.
Isaac Vanosdell
John Tinney
William Johnson
Thomas Slane
Samuel Slane
Daniel Slane
Benjamin Slane
Thomas Edwards
John Scott
James Sargeats
John Boxwell
Amos Day
Samuel Sutton
William Borer
Thomaston Powell
Horace Powell

John Powell
Benjamin Kidd
William Nixon
William Scott
John Millison
David Combs
New York
Luther Chamberlain
Lewis Chamberlain
[illegible]
William Bag
E. Moore
Thomas Egliston
Dr. Silas E. Merrill
Nash Shaketson
Kentucky
John Johnson
John Coyle
Asa Berle
_____ Stringer
Ohio
Thomas Fargo
John King
Van Gump
William Clayton
Pennsylvania
_____ Sheppard
_____ Robinson
Europe
Lawless
Patrick Malvary
Murphy Kingsmill
John Daly
Edward Barfoot
William Barfoot
Adam Barfoot

Appendix B

Lewis Coolidge's Letter to His Nephew,
William Dawes Coolidge, June 11, 1843

Spring Hill, Illinois
June 11, 1843
My Dear William,[1]

I have just now received your interesting and most welcome letter dated
N.Y., April 12. I do indeed feel mortified in being so unpardonly negligent in
writing you. It is a natural weakness, therefore you must forgive me. I wrote
you twice during the past winter but the terrible severity of the weather and its
concomitant circumstances must have prevented them from coming to hand.
Most devotedly and seriously do I thank our Heavenly Father for your good
health and happiness. May we prove our gratitude by living within his divine
precepts. I am happy to say we are all continuing in good health, allowing for
my entering the 'seas and yellow leaf' of the season of our pilgrimage.

My greatest solicitude and prayer to God is to live to see my dear children
established; then I think, I should depart in peace. Edward is now 19, a stout
athletic fellow and my main dependency. You may be surprised to learn that he
is now nearly six feet tall, a height not peculiar to our family. Ellen is eleven, a
fine brunette with eyes like the gazelle. Emma, 9 with flaxen hair and eyes like
the violet, this is my pet and failing. As I am the last who gets up in the morning, she always waits to eat breakfast with me, combs my hair and is ever 'artful in the attempts' to please me. I endeavor to motivate into their minds the
true consciousness of independence, which labour and an ignorance of the
vain appendage, falsely called luxuries, give to those who are far separated from
the refinements of the city. Here in these remote shades, hopefully they can
have no remembrance of slights or wrongs, no longing for society, nor irrita-
tion from the desires of unattainable distinctions. God in his mercy, grant they
may never be induced to mimic the vices to which they were not born, and
attempt the coarse covering of cunning and violence, for practices, which is a
science and frequently an object of education to conceal by petty elegances.

Pardon my severity of the city. I ever dislike it, altho I drew my first breath in it. I despise its aristocracy of wealth with its sequent sycophancy. I positively would prefer lodgment among the rocky mountains than to be obliged to reside in Beacon Street. I have been quite cavalierly treated by the "families" and it is now verified by my not running an announcement of one of my "betters" death by one of his immediate family! A duty owed to his memory and a proper respect to his only brother, the last of his father's house.[2]

The past winter has been of prodigious severity. It commenced on the 15 of Nov. and continued with "storms and tempests" and the most severe cold temperatures until April. To give you some idea of its rigour, more than ⅔ of all the winter wheat in the Western counties ruined. I have been obliged to cut down to the ground all my fine peach trees—nearly 50. Four years old and almost 5 inches in diameter, they were literally frozen to the roots, and consequently perished. This I mention as a very remarkable and singular feature of the effects of the past desolate and terrible winter. The farmers have been obliged to plough up the remains of their winter wheat for replacement by spring wheat, a grain of inferior quality. In consequence, winter wheat has advanced in price from 30 cents to 62 cents and will probably reach 75 cents before harvest.

I send you a sample of the paper in which you will perceive how low any kind of produce is here. I have never heard of such deplorable hard times. I had to sell my flax for $150, which amount was barely sufficient to clothe my family. I still "hope against hope" that I may, one of these days, be able to purchase a few sheep which would improve the possibilities of our getting a little clothing. But the wolves make dreadful havoc among them. Altho not as bad as a few years ago when I lost 4 one night and a short time afterward, all the remaining ones. I am comparatively grateful that while my neighbors, with few exceptions, lost some of their cattle because of the severity of the weather or lack of fodder; I have not lost one. Wheat, the food staple of the country has been the only article which has commanded cash the past winter, but at a price which would hardly pay to carry it to market, maybe 25 cents a bushel. All the other grains along with pork, beef or butter will not command cash at any price. This has meant an enormous loss to the farms with a return of only 20 to 30% of normal. [indecipherable line] Coffee and sugar have been for some time luxuries beyond our reach as they can be purchased with cash only— indeed little or no credit is given at Peoria for any thing we have available. Three years ago I made out to purchase all my groceries from the return of accommodating travelers that stopped at my house. Now very few call and those who do have no money in the morning! And I am obliged to put it down to expense. This is indeed vexatious but what can I do? I very seldom have a "quarter" and surely a dollar would be something I would scarcely recognize. However, "God will take care of us all."

I most deeply regret hearing such sad accounts of Frank.[3] He is greatly connected in my fine association particularly as he is the only one of his family, I regret to say, that has shown me common courtesy. I never received a line from any of them since my departure from Vermont, except from Frank, which was a mere letter of inquiry! As I am the only brother of their sainted mother (whose gentle virtues are fresh in my remembrances), it is passing strange they cannot afford to give me a thought, to one so closely connected. I rec'd a letter from Frank about 2 months since. It was obviously written under some abstraction of mind. It is dated "Brook's Farm" which I suppose in plain parlance means "a place for the snake," a strange seclusion indeed, producing, if any, the most bitter fruit! He observes, "We live as we please, do what we please and dress as we please. I have adopted a green and black plaid, as I think my ancestors were from Scotland and have chosen as an employment drawing and designing. I am now finishing two sketches which I intend sending you when finished. I like this place much, we live in common 'male and female.'" In another part of the letter he writes, "I have my fireplace ornamented with a deer's head made of moss in imitation of yours which hangs on your chimney. I do not despair of seeing you again in Illinois and chasing once more the deer over the plains." Poor fellow! I am induced to wish that he was in another and better world for I believe this to be one of peculiar suffering to him. You surprise me by mentioning in your letter that he had left Brook's Farm in miserable health, and is now staying with a physician in Vermont and trying to be restored, of which you had but little hope. Ah, my dear William, I sincerely hope his Merciful Father will take him to himself.[4]

The accounts you might have heard about the Bishop by the Farleys are all fidget! Frank was indeed obliged to sell to pay his own and his brother Charles' debts. The land originally cost him $200 and he sold it to the Bishop for $1400. It was thrice more valuable to the Bishop than to any other person; it being in the center of the college lawn and therefore indispensably necessary that it should be attached to it. The fact is that on the first arrival of Charles at this place, he appeared strongly anxious that Frank should remove to Audubon, Montgomery County near Alton where Charles had been preaching and where he [Charles] had contracted a considerable debt. He prevailed upon Frank to sell to the Bishop with the selfish and sole object of being himself placed in funds to liquidate his debts. To my certain knowledge, Frank paid $200 for this purpose with $100 more for his passage to Boston, besides which he paid nearly a year's board for Charles and wife while at Audubon. He also let Cartes have $100 which with what he owed and [indecipherable] assumed for Charles reduced his original fortune—his salvation— to nearly one half. With this, however, he could have done well had he remained with me and purchased 80 acres (which would have been quite sufficient for all his purposes) adjoining me, which I advised him with the greatest persuasion to do, but instead so bent was he to confide in Charles' sophistry and selfish projects and with this balance purchased a place in Audubon, built a house, and purchased an additional yoke of oxen. The cost of which was not less than $80. And finally after Charles' departure he was taken sick. To his chagrin and disappointment, no doubt, Frank finally was obliged to give up and sell his farm (not paid for yet, I believe) and after staying nearly a year at a Mrs. Townsend's, at great expense for his keep and physicians' attendance, took his departure for the East, leaving his affairs in status quo or in such a state that I think he will never realize one dollar to his advantage. So that you must perceive that all the fuss about the Bishop's cheating is false and you may be assured that the Bishop does not descend so low. It's surely a ruse to avoid reprehension by other persons. Besides, Frank's, Charles's and Cartes's conduct was outrageous—They indeed deceived him and took every advantage of his accommodating and generous comportment and then threw or attempted to throw the blame on the Bishop!

I am happy in informing you that the Bishop's college has improved the value of land in this vicinity. It should be reasonable that an institution and chapel of this kind must tend to introduce more refined society among us. The west wing will be finished this ensuing summer. This with the Chapel, professors' and students' rooms will cover an area of 2 acres. It will make a splendid appearance being built of stone in the Gothic style. The Chapel in the east wing is strictly Gothic, has a tower with corbels surmounted with a cross. It has an organ, two desks with a fine altar and vestibule. The pews are of oak in Gothic color. We have the delight of hearing in the solitude "the sweet subtle bells," and every day at morning and evening prayers, the solemn sounds float sweetly over the woods. A more enchanting situation for a seminary and chapel cannot be imagined. It is situated on high ground, surrounded by romantic, conical bluffs and ancient oaks with the Kichapoo "winding its devious way" in front, where but a few years ago the solemn trails were only trodden by the roving Indians. Before long they will be marked by the Pilgrim's staff and watered by his tears.

About 2 years past I cut an avenue through the woods so as to have a view of the Chapel. I believe I sent your sainted father a sketch with our own cottage. This view through the woods of nearly a mile is greatly admired. It cost me a great deal of labor, but I am abundantly repaid. Nothing you have around

Boston is so romantic! In the distant Sun, the Chapel appears like an abbey or ancient castle. It is rather too much shaded in Summer by trees in front of the Chapel, but the tower and narrow Gothic windows are more partially seen.

The Bishop insists that all festivals and fasts be sacredly kept. Last Christmas Eve, the Chapel was illuminated. It indeed made a beautiful appearance. The interior was dressed with evergreen and the sweet tones of the organ played by the Bishop's daughter, the solemn chorus, the melancholy pervading, the lectures and kindred associations and reflections almost melted me.

You must know, dear William, that a few days before Christmas, I was confirmed by the Bishop, and am now a communicant. My dear Amanda was confirmed a year previous and the children baptized. I now belong to the vestry and am a warden of the church. My former sentiments which were mainly superficial in respecting religious beliefs, was liberal and inclined to Unitarianism, but I always supported the established church, its Divine Litany and its spirit of pure devotion. May the Grace of God incline all our hearts to do His will "with a right spirit within us," and finally being led to Glory with our kindred Saints in Heavens.

You ask if you can do anything to serve me. Indeed, Heaven knows how grateful I am for your kind and affectionate feelings. All I can ask is to send, if in your power, any article you may not want from your wardrobe. I find it extremely difficult in these hard and increasingly pressing times to obtain clothing. Articles of the poorest quality are not to be had here without paying a great price, and now that our wheat has failed, the prospects are extremely gloomy. Should you be able, and I doubt not your good deportation, to send us a box, you will please to direct it to the care of Curtinious Griswold, forwarding Merchant, Peoria, Illinois.

What more shall I say but to commend you to that pure and perfect spirit who is the Father of us all. Give my most affectionate regards to your dear wife and kiss the little one for me.

Has Matilda arrived?[5] She can now plume herself on seeing what thousands have not—the ocean in all its majestic grandeur. I can easily sympathize with her feelings, the "Monstrous Waves" being once my home, and rolling on its surface being as familiar as my [indecipherable]. I should be delighted to have a little journal of her voyages. Hope she and the Captain[6] are well. It is most time for him to heave his mainsail to the mast, retire and live rusticly.

Ever your affectionate uncle,
L. Coolidge

P.S. Is Lady Hammond living?[7] and how is the Austin Family?[8]

Notes

Introduction

1. George Granville Putnam, *Salem Vessels and Their Voyages* (Salem, Mass.: Essex Institute, 1925) 83.

2. Mary Malloy, *"Boston Men" on the Northwest Coast: The American Maritime Fur Trade, 1788–1844* (Kingston, Ontario: Limestone Press, 1998) 70–71.

3. Andrew Delbanco, *Melville: His World and Work* (New York: Alfred A. Knopf, 2005) 17.

4. Lewis Gannett's introduction to *The Sea Wolf* (1904; New York: Bantam, 1960) ix.

Chapter 1: Lewis Coolidge's Journal

1. *Castle.* Castle Island, two miles from Boston, near the old harbor below South Boston. It was the site of defenses built by Boston's first settlers and the site of succeeding forts. The new Fort Independence was dedicated by President John Adams in 1799 and would have been there when the *Amethyst* passed by in 1806.

2. *Boston lighthouse.* The one now called the Outer Light, built in 1783 after a previous one there built in 1716 was destroyed in the Revolution. It is on Beacon Island, eight miles from the city.

3. *St. Nicholas.* St. Nicholas Island, off the west coast of Africa, in the Cape Verde group, about 18 degrees N. Latitude.

4. *Island of St. Iago.* In Cape Verdes, about 15 degrees N. Lat.

5. *Island of Trinadada.* Almost due south of the Cape Verdes in the South Atlantic, northeast of Rio de Janeiro.

6. *Goughs Island.* Gough Island today, a British possession in the South Atlantic.

7. *Swifttures.* Swifter, the forward shroud of the lower mast, one of a set of ropes used to support a mast.

8. *preventer shrouds.* Additional ropes to strengthen and support another rope.

9. *handed.* To hand a sail is to furl it.

10. *drifted.* Was carried at random by the force of the wind.

11. *Storm Staysail.* Small sail of very stout canvas, to be used in heavy weather.

12. *Cunn'd.* Conned. To direct the steerage of a vessel.

13. *Patagonia.* Old name for a region in South America, now mostly in Argentina.

14. *Sheet Anchor.* The largest of all anchors, a spare kept for great emergency. Vessels with a burden of fewer than 200 tons are not furnished with them.

15. *Cynthia.* The moon.

16. *"Come hither all Ye Epicurian Blades."* Presumably this is a reference to Shakespeare's *Antony and Cleopatra,* when Cleopatra calls for "Epicurean cooks" to "sharpen with cloyless sauce his [Antony's] appetite," act 2, scene 1.

17. *H[d].* Hogsheads.

18. *Coast of New Albion.* The name given to the Pacific coast of North America in 1579 by Sir Francis Drake.

19. *Saint Banca.* Presumably Punta Eugenia, Baja California Sur.

20. *Island of Cerros.* Cedros Island, off the coast of Baja California near Sebastian Viscaino Bay.

21. *CHATTERTON.* Thomas Chatterton, the English boy poet, 1752–1770. The quotation that follows, however, is credited to James Beattie, Scottish poet and essayist, 1735–1803.

22. *REUBENS.* Peter Paul Rubens, Flemish painter, 1577–1640.

23. *"Beauty sleeping in the lap of horror."* Line from Ann Radcliffe's *Mysteries of Udolpho* but according to a footnote in the Penguin Classics edition, more properly credited to William Gilpin, "The Castle of Indolence," canto 2, stanza 3.

24. *Thompson.* James Thomson, Scottish poet, 1700–1748.

25. *Patchen.* Likely a reference to Second Officer Thompson Patching, mentioned on page 10, who was the "President" of the *Amethyst's* Guadeloupe sealing party. Coolidge neglected to include Patching/Patchen in his crew list at the end of his journal.

26. *My hut.* Briton Cooper Busch included Lewis Coolidge's description of his hut in his excellent *The War against the Seals: A History of the North American Seal Fishery* as an indication of the harsh living conditions faced by sealing parties.

27. *"Honest Water."* From Shakespeare's *Timon of Athens:* "Here's that which is too weak to be a sinner, Honest water, which ne'er left man i' the mire," act 1, scene 2.

28. *"that bourne where no traveler returns."* From Shakespeare's *Hamlet:* "the dread of something after death, the undiscovered country, from whose bourne No traveller returns," act 3, scene 1.

29. *"without a pilot, and without a guide."* Presumably this is a reference to Samuel Johnson's *Journey to the Western Isles of Scotland:* "Whatever is imaged in the wildest tale, if giants, dragons, and enchantment be excepted, would be felt by him, who, wandering in the mountains without a guide, or upon the sea without a pilot, should be carried amidst his terror and uncertainty, to the hospitality and elegance of Raasay or Dunvegan."

30. *Sciotts.* Presumably the word here is *Scot* and refers to the Scottish poet Robert Burns.

31. *Proteus.* This likely should be Portius rather than Protius in reference to the great friendship between Portius and Marcus in Addison's *Cato.* However, the quote following this reference is from Oliver Goldsmith.

32. *"Oh Friendship thou fond soother of the human breast. . . ."* From Oliver Goldsmith's *Letters from a Citizen of the World,* letter 27.

33. *"without a Stone."* From Pope's "Elegy to the Memory of an Unfortunate Lady."

34. *"O'er Him. . . ."* From William Collins's "Ode to a Lady on the Death of Colonel Ross in the Action of Fontonoy."

35. *"Sea Elephant."* Usually referred as elephant seals.

36. *"resting our heads. . . ."* From Joseph Addison's *Cato*, act 1, scene 4.

37. *"On the first friendly Bank. . . ."* A paraphrase of Addison's "On the first friendly bank he throws him down."

38. *"streach the eager eye."* This reference is unknown.

39. *"Triumph"* The *Triumph* was built at Guilford, Connecticut, in 1805. Her master on this voyage was William Brintnall.

40. *St. Vare.* Believed to one of the islands in the Territory of the French Southern and Antarctic Lands (*Territoire des Terres australes et antarctiques françaises*), consisting of a group of volcanic islands in the southern Indian Ocean visited in the nineteenth century by whalers and sealers. Probably St. Paul.

41. *Port Jackson.* Today Sydney, New South Wales, Australia.

42. *Norfolk Island.* Island east of Australia between New Caledonia and New Zealand.

43. *Friendly Islands.* Now Tonga Islands, east of the Fijis, in the South Pacific.

44. *Pharsalia.* Coolidge either has the battle or the general mixed up. Caesar beat Pompey in a decisive battle at Pharsalus, Greece, in 48 B.C.

45. *"Bachus now set spurs to his steed."* This reference is unknown.

46. *Elop'd.* In the dictionary sense of running away from one's place or duty; the amorous sense also applies, however, elsewhere in this journal.

47. *St. Rosalie.* Probably Santa Rosa Island just above Los Angeles and not actually as far north as he says.

48. *St. Barbara.* A small island to the west of Santa Catalina Island.

49. *St. Catalina.* Today's Catalina Island.

50. *Todos Santos.* Ensenada de Todos Santos, first good harbor south of the border between California and Baja California.

51. *Deaux Anges.* According to the text, a village some thirty miles inland from the Bay of All Saints ("Todos Santos") in northern Baja California, Mexico. There is no record of a village in the Baja region of this name.

52. *"Death is an Eternal Sleep."* Said by Joseph Fouché, a strong supporter of regicide in the French Revolution, who was placed by his orders on the cemetery gates of France in 1794.

53. *Porto St. Pedro.* San Pedro Bay, Los Angeles County.

54. *hhkfs.* handkerchiefs.

55. *Gil Blas.* Hero of Le Sage's picaresque 1735 novel of the same name.

56. *Leathur not tan'd, and ornamented.* Apparently tooled leather.

57. *"spavin'd and shoulder Shotten."* Lamed, and with a sprained shoulder. The latter phrase is from Shakespeare's *Taming of the Shrew* (act 3, scene 2) but is also just an archaic phrase.

58. *St. Clements.* San Clemente Island, off the coast of California, between Los Angeles and San Diego.

59. *Oyhee.* Hawaii.

60. *Mowee.* Maui, Hawaiian Island.

61. *Warhoo/Wharhoo/Woahoo.* Oahu, Hawaii Island.

62. *Malahi.* Molokai, Hawaiian Island.

63. *"If after every Tempest. . . ."* Shakespeare's *Othello*, act 2, scene 1.

64. *Atooi.* Kauai, Hawaiian Island

65. *Island of Pian.* In all likelihood, this is Pagan Island in the Northern Mariana Islands chain, located at 18.10ffi N 145.76ffi E.

66. *Ladrone Islands.* Refers to the Marianas Islands, including Guam. The Spanish word for robber was applied to them because of their piratical inhabitants, who preyed on all passing ships.

67. *Bashee Islands.* Babuyan Islands, just north of the Philippines.

68. *ladrons.* Robbers, pirates.

69. *Linsa passage.* Probably Lindsay, for Lindsay Island, northwest of the Marianas and southeast of the Bashees (Babuyan Islands).

70. *sweeps.* Large oars used on small sailing ships.

71. *"haul'd their Wind."* Brought the ship's prow nearer the wind after she had been going free.

72. *Macoa.* Macao Island off southwest China, near Canton.

73. *Camboose.* Cast-iron cooking apparatus.

74. *Pingasanon.* Pangasinan Province on Luzon Island in the Philippines.

75. *Maravilles.* Either Mount Mariveles on Bataan or Corregidor Island itself.

76. *Island.* Corregidor.

77. *Pintadores.* A scombroid fish, its name comes from the Spanish and Portuguese *pintado*, meaning "painted."

78. *Olopodridas.* Ollapodrida is a well-known Spanish dish of meat and vegetable stew.

79. *Count Lishamogo and Squire Chumpio.* This reference is unknown.

80. *Beach a'la Mar.* Bêche-de-mer, literally "caterpillars of the sea," also known as trepang or sea cucumbers, found in Australia and the East Indies; they are typically boiled, dried and smoked. The Chinese use them for soup.

81. *came on board to press.* Impressment of sailors, a contributing cause of the War of 1812 between the United States and England.

82. *Acapulco.* Seaport on west coast of Mexico.

83. *Pulo Penang.* Island in the Straits of Malacca between Sumatra and the Malay Peninsula.

84. *Arrack.* Dutch East Indies drink of rum with fruit flavors.

85. *Pelew Isles.* Today called Palau.

86. *Streights of San Barnardino.* Channel between the extreme southeast tip of Luzon Island and the northwest tip of Samar Island. The ship was sailing eastward.

87. *Buleno.* Probably the present-day Bulan, city in Sorsogon province.

88. *Corora.* Today Koror, capital of Palau.

89. *wore Ship.* Veered, brought the vessel upon the other tack by turning her head away from the wind. Wearing causes the ship to lose ground, so is never practiced except when she will not tack, or where tacking might be dangerous.

90. *to stay the Ship.* To tack or go about.

91. *Rom.* Gypsy-like garment or *romal,* Indian kerchief.

92. *Cyprian Palaces.* Houses of prostitution, in reference to legendary licentious worship of Aphrodite, reputedly born on the island of Cyprus. *Cyprian* was the term especially used in the eighteenth and nineteenth centuries.

93. *tarro.* Taro, cultivated in the tropics for its edible starchy tuberous rootstock.

94. *matching.* Twisted tow, prepared with saltpeter and other flammable ingredients for firing the ship's guns.

95. *Swivels on the taffes rail.* Small guns on the taff rail, which extends across the stern.

96. *boarding Nettings.* A frame of stout nettings put around a ship to prevent her being boarded.

97. *"the better grace."* Probably intended to invoke a line from Shakespeare's *Twelfth Night:* "He does it with a better grace," act 2, scene 3.

98. *picol.* Picul, an Oriental commercial weight, from 133⅓ to 140 pounds.

99. *eclipse.* Occurred on April 4, 1810.

100. *"Wocosky."* This reference is unknown.

101. *Ground tackling.* A general name for anchors and cables used in anchoring or mooring vessels.

102. *unbent the sails.* Loosen and cast them from the yards, beams, or stays.

103. *Sway'd up.* Threw a strain on a mast rope and started the mast upwards, so that the fid may be taken out before lowering the mast. The fid is a piece of wood or iron made to go through the heel of an upper mast and rest on the trestletrees in order to keep the mast in its place.

104. *Latitude 16.15.135 E. Longitude.* Readings are apparently in error here by as much as five hundred miles; Luzon could not be sighted from that distance.

105. *Streights of Luzon.* Probably Babuyan Channel, just north of Luzon.

106. *St. Boxadore.* Cape Bojeador, on northwest tip of Luzon.

107. *Pedro Bianco. Pedra Branca* signifies "white stone" in Portuguese; today called Xiaosanmen Dao, an island due east of Hong Kong at 22'26" N, 114'38" E.

108. *Brandons Bay.* Brandon's Bay is now known as Honghai Bay and is located at 22'40" N, 115'10" E.

109. *Feukien Point.* In all likelihood Fokai Point, the point of land on the Chinese mainland at 22'37" N, 114'51" E.

110. *Grand Ladrone.* One of a group of islands in the China Sea opposite the entrance to the Canton River.

111. *NY. Evening Post.* Founded in 1801, the newspaper continued until the spring of 1942.

112. *Boca Tigres.* Bocca Tigris, a channel between the upper and lower Pearl Rivers, near Canton.

113. *"We are such stuff. . . ."* From Shakespeare's *Tempest,* act 4, scene 1.

114. *Streights of Banca.* Past the Bangka Island, northeast of lower Sumatra.

115. *Streights of Sunda.* Between Sumatra and Tava.

116. *Mala.* Malay.

117. *Cape St. Aguillas.* Cape Agulhas, southeast of the Cape of Good Hope. Agulhas is the southernmost tip of the African continent.

118. *St. Helena.* This was still four years before Napoleon's defeat and final exile here.

119. *E-I Company.* Presumably the East India Company.

120. *Cartel.* Ship used for exchange of prisoners.

121. *Conge ala Mode D. St. Cloud.* Ceremonious bows.

122. *"that uses power, but forgets right."* This reference is unknown.

123. *highlands of York.* The New Jersey Palisades, north of New York City.

CHAPTER 2: The Fur Seal Trade with China in the Early 1800s

1. Francis Ross Carpenter, *The Old China Trade: Americans in Canton, 1784–1843* (New York: Coward, McCann & Geoghan, 1976) 74.

2. Carpenter 14.

3. Samuel Eliot Morison, *The Maritime History of Massachusetts, 1783–1860* (1921; repr. Boston: Northeastern University Press, 1976) 44.

4. Samuel Eliot Morison, *By Land and by Sea* (New York: Alfred A. Knopf, 1954) 72.

5. Carpenter 130.

6. Sydney and Marjorie Greenbie, *Gold of Ophir* (New York: Doubleday, Page, and Company, 1925) 49.

7. Foster Rhea Dulles, *The Old China Trade* (Boston and New York: Houghton Mifflin, 1930) 96.

8. Conversation with Dr. David Pawson, senior research scientist at the National Museum of Natural History, Smithsonian Institution, Washington, D.C., on November 29, 2005.

9. The descriptions of fur seals, their populations, and their distributions draw heavily on three sources: Peter Reijinders et al., *Seals, Fur Seals, Sea Lions, and Walrus* (Gland, Switzerland: International Union for the Conservation of Nature and Natural Resources, 1993); International Union for the Conservation of Nature and Natural Resources, *Seals* (Gland, Switzerland: International Union for the Conservation of Nature and Natural Resources, 1995); and Phyllis Roberts Evans, *The Sea World Book of Seals and Sea Lions* (New York: Harcourt Brace Jovanovich, 1986).

10. Evans 10.

11. Carpenter 79.

12. Carpenter 125.

13. Fredericka Martin, *The Hunting of the Silver Fleece: Epic of the Fur Seal* (New York: Greenberg, 1946) 100–101.

14. Briton Cooper Busch, *The War against the Seals: A History of the North American Seal Fishery* (Kingston, Ontario: McGill-Queen's University Press, 1985) 6.

15. Martin, 101–102.

16. Dulles 106.

17. Dulles 110.

18. Dulles 110.

19. Shu-Lun Pan, *The Trade of the United States with China* (New York: China Trade Bureau, 1924) 12.

20. Shu-Lun Pan 17.

21. Thomas N. Layton, *The Voyage of the Frolic* (Stanford, Calif.: Stanford University Press, 1997) 28.

22. Shu-Lu Pan 9.

CHAPTER 3: The Lewis Coolidge Family

1. The paragraphs on the genealogy of Lewis Coolidge, including the lives of the immigrating ancestors, John and Mary Coolidge, and other early American Coolidges, draws heavily on Emma Downing Coolidge, *Descendants of John and Mary Coolidge of Watertown, Massachusetts, 1630* (Boston: Wright and Potter Printing Company, 1930).

2. Coolidge 31.

3. Coolidge 31.

4. Coolidge 32.

5. Frederick Coolidge Crawford, *One Branch of the Coolidge Family* (Cleveland: Privately printed, 1964) 8.

6. Coolidge 33.

7. Coolidge 329.

8. Coolidge 371.

9. Coolidge 357; and Samuel Eliot Morison, *The Oxford History of the American People.* (New York: Oxford University Press, 1965) 207.

10. Henry W. Holland, *William Dawes and His Ride with Paul Revere* (Boston: John Wilson and Son, 1878) 74.

11. James Truslow Adams, *The History of New England*, vol. 2, *Revolutionary New England: 1691–1776* (New York: Cooper Square, 1968) 304.

12. C. Burr Dawes, *William Dawes, First Rider for the Revolution* (Ohio: Historic Gardens Press, 1976) 167.

13. Dawes 167.

14. Holland 74.

15. Coolidge 358.

16. Coolidge 361.

17. The first mate on the *Lady Washington*, the companion ship to the *Columbia*, was Davis Coolidge, possibly a distant cousin of Lewis Coolidge. The second mate on the *Columbia* was Joseph Ingraham, also quite possibly a relative of Lewis through his

great-grandmother Hannah Ingram Coolidge. A. C. Laut, *Vikings of the Pacific* (New York: Macmillan, 1905) 214.

18. George Green Schackleford, ed., *Collected Papers to Commemorate Fifty Years of the Monticello Association of the Descendants of Thomas Jefferson* (Trenton, N.J.: Princeton University Press) 89.

19. Shackleford 89–90.

20. A pipe was "a large cask of varying capacity … [or] such a cask as a measure of capacity … [usually] 126 wine gallons." *Random House Dictionary of the English Language, 2nd Edition, Unabridged* (1983, New York: Random House, 1987) 1474.

21. M. V. B. Perley, compiler, *History and Genealogy of the Perley Family* (Salem, Mass.: Privately published, 1906) 203.

22. Phil Bensted, Bensted Home Pages, "Warship 'Curlew,'" available at http://users .qld.chariot.net.au/~dialabull/Others.htm, accessed July 28, 2008.

23. George Coggeshall, *History of the American Privateers, and Letters-of-Marque, During Our War with England in the Years 1812, '13, and '14* (New York: Published by the author, 1856) 421.

24. Perley 203.

25. Samuel Eliot Morison, *The Maritime History of Massachusetts; 1783–1860* (1921; repr. Boston: Northeastern University Press, 1979) 199.

26. Jon E. Lewis, ed., *Life Before the Mast* (Edison, N.J.: Castle Books, 2002) 318.

27. Morison 200.

28. Stephen Howarth, *To Shining Sea: A History of the U. S. Navy, 1775–1991* (New York: Random House, 1991) 13.

29. "Coolage [*sic*], Lewis: Prisoner 2277. Rank: Seaman. From: *Nolante* [*sic*], Merchant Vessel. Captured: 26 Mar 1813 at sea by *HMS Curlew* Interned: 04 Apr 1813 Discharged 02 Jun 1813. Received from *HMS Curlew*. To Boston for exchange." Harrison Scott Baker II, transcriber, *American Prisoners of War Held at Halifax during the War of 1812: June 1812–April 1815*, vol. 1 (Willow Bend Books, 2005) 92.

30. As told to coauthor Evabeth Miller Kienast by Eleanor Jeannette Coolidge, ca. 1942.

31. Gardner W. Pearson, *Records of the Massachusetts Volunteer Militia: Called Out by the Governor of Massachusetts to Suppress a Threatened Invasion during the War of 1812–1814* (Boston: Wright and Potter Printing Co., 1913) 80.

32. H. P. Smith, ed., *History of Addison County, Vermont, with Illustrations and Biographical Sketches of Some of Its Prominent Men and Pioneers* (Syracuse, N.Y.: D. Mason & Co., 1886) 702–12.

33. Smith 712.

34. Jubilee College State Historic Site, "2002 Jubilee College State Historic Site Visitors and Event Guide," Brimfield, Illinois, 2002, 5–13.

35. Richard E. Morris, ed., *Encyclopedia of American History* (New York: Harper, 1953) 436–437.

36. Lewis Coolidge, "Coolidge Settlement," *Peoria Register and North-Western Gazeteer* December 2, 1837, 1.

37. Lewis Coolidge, letter to Charles Dawes Coolidge, June 4, 1843.

38. Elmer Hall Palmer, *Genealogical Record of the Descendants of Walter Palmer*, vol. 1, *Eight Generations* (N.p.:Walter Palmer Society, 2002) 354.

APPENDIX B

1. We are indebted to Austin V. Felt for the transcription of this letter with its miniscule handwriting. The addressee is Lewis Coolidge's nephew, William Dawes Coolidge, the son of Lewis's elder brother William, who was a merchant in Boston and Baltimore.

It is difficult to understand how this letter remained with the Coolidge family in the Midwest as it was postmarked in Peoria, Illinois, and presumably mailed to William Coolidge in Boston. One possibility is that the letter was undeliverable for some reason and returned to Lewis Coolidge in Peoria County, Illinois, where it remained with his family.

2. Presumably this is a reference to the March 17, 1842, death of Lewis's brother, Charles Dawes Coolidge, a Boston merchant.

3. A reference to Frank Dennison Farley, the son of Lewis's sister Lydia Coolidge Farley.

4. While at Brook Farm, Frank Farley was regarded as an integral member of that society in a letter written on April 26, 1841, from Elizabeth Palmer Peabody to fellow transcendentalist Rev. John S. Dwight. This letter was reprinted in an article by Zoltan Haraszti entitled "Brook Farm As Revealed by Unpublished Letters In the Boston Public Library," which appeared in the February and March 1937 issues of *More Books, the Bulletin of the Boston Public Library entitled Brook Farm as Revealed by Unpublished Letters in the Boston Public Library.* Ms. Peabody wrote, "In a fortnight, [Nathaniel] Hawthorne and Mr. Warren Burton joined them [George and Sophia Ripley, William Allen, and Elise Barker], and Hawthorne has taken hold with the greatest spirit and proves a fine workman. But Frank Farley is the crown of all. He knows how to do every species of work, from cooking and other kinds of domestic labour through all the processes of farming and dealing with live stock; and solaces his leisure hours with the fine arts—for he draws—and reads aloud with histrionic beauty." Haraszti noted that Nathaniel Hawthorne wrote in his *Note Books* on April 14, 1841, "After breakfast, Mr. Ripley put a four-pronged instrument into my hands, which he gave me to understand was called a pitchfork; and he and Mr. Farley being armed with similar weapons, we all three commenced a gallant attack upon a heap of manure." Lewis Coolidge needn't have worried about Frank Farley's immediate health. After this letter was written, Frank Farley lived another eighteen years, married, and had children.

5. Matilda Curtis Coolidge, sister of William Dawes Coolidge and niece of Lewis Coolidge.

6. Matilda's husband George James Curtis, a captain of merchant ships.

7. Presumably Elizabeth Coolidge Hammond Coolidge, born 1767, the daughter of Jonas and Anna Coolidge who married Jonathan Hammond. He died in 1807, and Elizather then married her distant cousin Gen. Jonathan Coolidge.

8. Presumably the family of Benjamin and Jane Austin of Boston. Their daughter Eliza married Lewis Coolidge's younger brother, Charles Dawes Coolidge.

BIBLIOGRAPHY

Adams, James Truslow. *The History of New England,* vol. 2, *Revolutionary New England: 1691–1776.* New York: Cooper Square, 1968.

Bauer, K. Jack. *A Maritime History of the United States: The Role of America's Seas and Waterways.* Columbia: Unversity of South Carolina, 1988.

Beard, Charles A., and Mary R Beard. *The Rise of American Civilization.* 1927; New York: Macmillan, 1944.

Bogart, Ernest Ludlow. *Economic History of the American People.* New York: Longmans, Green, 1932.

Boynton, Henry Walcott. *James Fenimore Cooper.* New York: Frederick Ungar, 1966.

Busch, Briton Cooper. *The War against the Seals: A History of the North American Seal Fishery.* Kingston, Ontario: McGill-Queen's University Press; Gloucester: A. Sutton, 1985.

Carpenter, Francis Ross. *The Old China Trade: Americans in Canton, 1784–1843.* New York: Coward, McCann, and Geoghan, 1976.

Clark, William H. *Ships and Sailors: The Story of Our Merchant Marine.* Boston: L. C. Page, 1938.

Coggeshall, George. *History of the American Privateers and Letters-of-Marque, during Our War with England in the Years 1812, '13, and '14.* New York: Privately published by the author, 1856.

Coolidge, Emma Downing. *Descendants of John and Mary Coolidge of Watertown, Massachusetts, 1630.* Boston: Wright and Potter Printing Company, 1930.

Coolidge, Harold Jefferson, and Robert Howard Lord. *Archibald Cary Coolidge: Life and Letters.* Boston: Houghton Mifflin, 1932.

Coolidge, T. Jefferson. *The Autobiography of T. Jefferson Coolidge, 1831–1920.* Boston: Houghton Mifflin, 1923.

Cooper, James Fenimore. *The Sea Lions; or, The Lost Sealers.* 1843; repr., Whitefish, Mont.: Kessinger Publishing, 2004.

Crawford, Frederick Coolidge. *One Branch of the Coolidge Family.* Cleveland: Privately printed, 1964.

Crawford, Mary Caroline. *Famous Families of Massachusetts.* Boston: Little, Brown, 1930.

Dana, Richard Henry. *Two Years before the Mast.* 1869; New York: Signet, 1964.

Delbanco, Andrew. *Melville: His World and Work.* New York: Alfred A. Knopf, 2005.

DeVoto, Bernard, ed. *The Journals of Lewis and Clark.* Boston: Houghton Mifflin, 1953.

Dawes, C. Burr. *William Dawes, First Rider for the Revolution.* Ohio: Historic Gardens Press, 1976.

Dorr, Sullivan. "The Sullivan Dorr Papers." Rhode Island Historical Society Library, Providence, Rhode Island.

Dudden, Arthur Power. *The American Pacific: From the Old China Trade to the Present.* New York: Oxford University, 1992.

Dulles, Foster Rhea. *The Old China Trade.* Boston and New York: Houghton Mifflin, 1930.

Eldridge, Frank R. *Trading with Asia.* New York: D. Apleton, 1929.

Elliott, Henry W. *Report on the Seal Islands of Alaska.* Washington: Government Printing Office, 1884.

Evans, Phyllis Roberts. *The Sea World Book of Seals and Sea Lions.* New York: Harcourt Brace Jovanovich, 1986.

Fairbank, John King. *The United States and China.* 4th ed. Cambridge, Mass.: Harvard University, 1979.

Fairbank, John King. *Trade and Diplomacy on the China Coast: The Opening of the Treaty Ports, 1842–1854.* 1953; repr. Stanford, California: Stanford University, 1969.

Fanning, Edmund. *Voyages and Disoveries in the South Seas; 1792–1832.* 1924; repr. New York: Dover, 1989.

———. *Voyages to the South Seas, Indian and Pacific Oceans, China Sea, North-West Coast, Feejee Islands, South Shetlands, &c.* 1838; repr. Upper Saddle River, N.J.: Gregg Press, 1970.

Farrar, Victor J. *The Purchase of Alaska.* Washington: W. F. Roberts, 1935.

Felt, Joseph Barlow. *Annals of Salem.* 2 vols. 1845; repr. Salem: Higginson, 2005.

Ford, Alice, ed. *Audubon, by Himself.* Garden City, N.Y.: Natural History Press, 1969.

Fuess, Claude M. *Calvin Coolidge: The Man from Vermont.* Hamden, Conn.: Archon, 1965.

Garitee, James R. *The Republic's Private Navy: The American Privateering Business as Practiced by Baltimore during the War of 1812.* Middletown, Conn.: Wesleyan University Press, 1977.

Gilman, Carolyn. *Lewis and Clark: Across the Divide.* Washington, D.C.: Smithsonian Books, 2003.

Greenbie, Sydney, and Marjorie Greenbie. *Gold of Ophir.* New York: Doubleday, Page, and Co., 1925.

Greenberg, Michael. *British Trade and the Opening of China, 1800–1842.* Cambridge, U.K.: Cambridge University, 1951.

Gregory, J. S. *Great Britain and the Taipings.* New York: Frederick A. Praeger, 1969.

Griffin, Eldon. *Clippers and Consuls: American Consular and Commercial Relations with Eastern Asia, 1845–1860.* Ann Arbor, Mich.: Edwards Brothers, 1938.

Hanes, W. Travis, and Frank Sanello. *The Opium Wars: The Addiction of One Empire and the Corruption of Another.* Naperville, Ill.: Sourcebooks, 2002.

Haraszti, Zoltan. "Brook Farm as Revealed by Unpublished Letters in the Boston Public Library." *More Books, the Bulletin of the Boston Public Library.* February and March 1937.

Holland, Henry W. *William Dawes and His Ride with Paul Revere*. Boston: John Wilson and Son, 1878.

Howarth, Stephen, *To Shining Sea: A History of the United States Navy, 1775–1991*. New York: Random House, 1991.

Howay, F. W., ed. *The Dixon-Meares Controversy*. Toronto and New York: Ryerson Press / L.Carrier & Co., 1929?.

International Union for the Conservation of Nature and Natural Resources. *Seals*. Gland, Switzerland: International Union for the Conservation of Nature and Natural Resources, 1995.

Johnson, Paul. *A History of the American People*. New York: Harper Collins, 1997.

Jones, Landon Y., ed. *The Essential Lewis and Clark*. New York: Ecco Press, 2000.

Laing, Alexander. *The American Heritage History of Seafaring America*. New York: American Heritage, 1974.

Lathem, Edward Connery, ed. *Meet Calvin Coolidge, the Man behind the Myth*. Brattleboro, Vt.: Stephen Greene Press, 1960.

Laut, A. C. *Vikings of the Pacific: The Adventures of the Explorers Who Came from the West, Eastward*. New York: Macmillan, 1905.

Layton, Thomas N. *The Voyage of the Frolic*. Stanford, Calif.: Stanford University Press, 1997.

Leach, Paul R. *That Man Dawes*. Chicago: Reilly and Lee, 1930.

Lewis, Jon E., ed. *Life before the Mast: Sailors' Eyewitness Accounts from the Age of Fighting Ships*. Edison, N.J.: Castle, 2002.

London, Jack. *The Sea Wolf*. 1904; repr. New York: Bantam, 1960.

Maclay, Edgar Stanton, *A History of American Privateers*. 1899; repr. Freeport, N.Y.: Books for Libraries Press, 1970.

Malloy, Mary. *Boston Men on the Northwest Coast: The American Fur Trade, 1788–1844*. Kingston, Ontario: Limestone Press, 1998.

Martin, Fredericka. *The Hunting of the Silver Fleece: Epic of the Fur Seal*. New York: Greenberg, 1946.

McCann, Thomas P. *An American Company: The Tragedy of United Fruit*. New York: Crown, 1976.

Meares, John. *Voyages Made in the Years 1788 and 1789 from China to the North-West Coast of America*. 1789; repr. New York: Da Capo Press, 1967.

Melville, Herman. "Benito Cereno." In *Billy Budd and Other Tales*. New York: Signet Classics, 1979.

———. *Omoo*. 1847; Mineola, N.Y.: Dover, 2000.

Michener, James A. *Alaska*. New York: Ballantine, 1988.

———. *Hawaii*. New York: Random House, 1959.

Morison, Samuel Eliot. *By Land and By Sea*. New York: Alfred A. Knopf, 1954.

———. *The Maritime History of Massachusetts: 1783–1860*. 1921; repr. Boston: Northeastern University Press, 1979.

———. *The Oxford History of the American People*. New York: Oxford University Press, 1965.

Morris, Richard E., ed. *Encyclopedia of American History.* New York: Harper, 1953.

Ogden, Adele, *The California Sea Otter Trade: 1784–1848.* Berkeley and Los Angeles: University of California Press, 1941.

Okun, S. B. *The Russian American Company.* Cambridge, Mass.: Harvard University Press, 1951.

Palmer, Elmer Hall. *Genealogical Record of the Descendants of Walter Palmer,* vol. 1, *Eight Generations.* Walter Palmer Society, 2002.

Pan, Shu-Lun. *The Trade of the United States with China.* New York: China Trade Bureau, 1924.

Pawson, David L. et al. *Sea Stars, Sea Urchins, and Allies.* Washington, D.C.: Smithsonian, 1995.

Philbrick, Nathaniel. *In the Heart of the Sea: The Tragedy of the Whaleship Essex.* New York: Viking, 2000.

Quennell, Peter. *Byron, a Self-Portrait: Letters and Diaries, 1798–1824.* Vol. 2. New York: Humanities Press, 1967.

Radcliffe, Ann. *The Mysteries of Udolpho.* 1794; repr. New York: Penguin, 2001.

Reijinders, Peter, et al. *Seals, Fur Seals, Sea Lions, and Walrus.* Gland, Switzerland: International Union for the Conservation of Nature and Natural Resources, 1993.

Schackleford, George Green, ed. *Collected Papers to Commemorate Fifty Years of the Monticello Association of the Descendants of Thomas Jefferson.* Trenton, N.J.: Princeton University Press.

Schurman, Franz, and Orville Schell, eds. *Imperial China: The Decline of the Last Dynasty and the Origins of Modern China.* 1954; repr. New York: Vintage, 1967.

Seagraves, Eleanor Roosevelt, ed. *Delano's Voyages of Commerce and Discovery: Amaso Delano in China, the Pacific Islands, Australia, and South America, 1789–1807.* 1817; repr. Stockbridge, Mass.: Berkshire House, 1994.

Smith, H. P., ed. *History of Addison County, Vermont, with Illustrations and Biographical Sketches of Some of Its Prominent Men and Pioneers.* Syracuse, N.Y.: D. Mason and Co., 1886.

Slaughter, Thomas P. *Exploring Lewis and Clark.* New York: Alfred A. Knopf, 2003.

Steele, A. T. *The American People and China.* New York: McGraw Hill, 1966.

Strong, Charles S. *The Story of American Sailing Ships.* New York: Grosset and Dunlap, 1957.

Williams, Edward Thomas. *China: Yesterday and To-Day.* 1923; repr. New York: Thomas Y. Crowell, 1928.

Williams, S. Wells, *The Middle Kingdom: A Survey of the Geography, Government, Literature, Social Life, Arts, and History of the Chinese Empire and Its Inhabitants.* New York: Charles Scribner's Sons, 1883.

"2002 Jubilee College State Historic Site Visitors and Event Guide." Peoria, Ill., 2002.

Index

Page numbers in italic type indicate photographs, maps, or illustrations.

About the Editors

A native of central Illinois, EVABETH MILLER KIENAST (1912–2007) was a reporter and arts columnist from 1934 to 1959 for the *Peoria Star*, where she worked with Lewis Coolidge's granddaughter, who first introduced her to his maritime diary. Plans to publish her transcription of the diary in book form were delayed for six decades until communication with John Phillip Felt renewed interest in the project and led to the present volume.

Also an Illinois native, JOHN PHILLIP FELT is the great-great-grandson of Lewis Coolidge. Felt served as an officer in the U.S. Navy and as a foreign service officer in the U.S. State Department. Now retired, he lives in Alexandria, Virginia. He and his wife, Judy, have two children.